My Organis ion i Jungle

Jef Staes

My Organisation is a Jungle

lannoo campus

Red Monkey® and Engine of Innovation® are registered marks
of FeNESTRA bvba, Herentals, Belgium

D/2008/45/269 – ISBN 978 90 209 7712 7 – NUR 801/807

DESIGN & COVER Elke Feusels, Peer De Maeyer & Studio Lannoo
© Jef Staes, Publishinghouse LannooCampus, Leuven, 2008

Publishinghouse LannooCampus
Naamsesteenweg 201
B-3001 Leuven
www.lannoocampus.com

Contents

PART II · AN ANSWER TO THE 3D CHALLENGE:
RED MONKEY® POLITICS

....

PART III · RED MONKEY® INNOVATION MANAGEMENT IN THE 3D-ORGANISATION

....

The world is not controlled by laws of certainty, but by laws of probability and possibilities. We are living in a transitional period toward a society of information and that requires a new vocabulary. I think people tend to use terms like 'chaos' and 'self-organisation' superficially but at least it's going in the right direction. The Internet is a self-organisation. It's an example of something spontaneous, something beyond traditional approaches... and it works!

Ilya Prigogine, father of the chaos theory
(*Knack* magazine 28-29, 2007)

The birth of the Internet could only have been possible in a 'public' environment. In a commercial company, two nerds like Tim Berners-Lee and I never would have had the freedom to experiment freely.

Robert Caillau, co-inventor of the world-wide web
(*Knack* magazine 28-29; 2007)

My thanks to...

My family, who had to do without me while I was once again submerged in my passion;

My former 2D and 3D-managers, who illustrated the difference between 2D and 3D;

Paul, Jan and everyone else who helped me to unravel my chaotic thoughts;

Bart, Les and Niel, who assisted me in making this book available in English;

The inspiring people of the Engine of Innovation® May 2004 Consortium;

You, the reader, who will brake for Red Monkeys from now on.

Preface

My Organisation is a Jungle. I have been considering this title for quite some time. It's the result of fifteen years of experience as a training manager, Corporate Learning Officer and advisor on organisational development.

There is just a touch of despair in that title – at least, there is for those who feel defeated by the fact that each organisation is, in essence, a jungle. However, those who accept this jungle as a given and work with it, will see this title as a positive challenge. Holders of both perspectives can benefit from reading this book, provided they understand how the jungle works and how it changes. You will not only learn the hard laws of the jungle – how jungle creatures hunt and kill – but also how you can use this knowledge to your advantage.

This last question is by far the most interesting and will be the main focus of the book. Change is of absolute importance in organisations these days. Even so...

After all my years of working in and with different companies, I have reached the conclusion that organisations are failing to evolve into innovative and learning organisations, driven by people who are passionate about their job. For years, the business world has been talking about the need and the urgency for cultural change – but it just doesn't happen. Millions are invested in education, training, management courses and master programmes ... but to no avail. After all this effort, organisations are still very much the way they were twenty years ago.

In some respects, my views in this book will be challenging. The contrast between black-and-white is clearest and helps to explain matters more pointedly. I will not focus on the question of how a company can achieve cultural change. Instead, I will offer the reader a chance to reflect. This is the first step in a continuous process which, over time, will turn your company into a truly dynamic organisation. The jungle will still be there, but diversity will be treated with more respect and will have a beneficial influence on your results. This book is an eye-opener for those who want to transform their organisation into a continuously changing and learning organisation.

I hope that this book will be an inspiring revelation which causes a torrent of insights and ideas, supported by the will to try and use them. If that is the case: welcome to the club! Welcome to the club of innovative organisations. The club of the future.

Jef Staes

Story line

The biggest challenge facing innovation today is neither creativity nor entrepreneurship; it is helping people to understand something that doesn't yet exist, something abstract. Although this abstraction already exists in the mind of its creator, the words and practical examples to provide clarity to others are still missing.

It is therefore important not to try too hard to prove that your ideas will work but to start by using your passion to convince other people to join you – and make them work. The only way to achieve this is by storytelling and metaphors.

The creation of a new type of organisations is the central theme of this story. Today's organisations try to be innovative but can't. They were conceived with the wrong mental models. What I am talking about is a new breed of organisations that doesn't yet exist: organisations built to innovate. And that is why I will have to use storytelling and metaphors.

This book will tell a story that will take you from the turbulent waves of the ocean to the dense foliage of the jungle. In Part I we will underline the need for a new type of organisation. The business environment has changed so much that we even need a new vocabulary to explain the differences. The terms '2D' and '3D' for example: 2D-organisations are organisations of the past and 3D-organisations are organisations of the future. To illustrate this,

I use the metaphor of a barge struggling to survive in unexplored, stormy waters. I guarantee that you will never again talk about 'an organisation' but will start talking about 2D and 3D-organisations.

Organisations cannot survive in fast moving 3D-environments without completely rethinking their process of innovation. Part II introduces the Red Monkey as a symbol for a radical and confrontational idea, trying to survive in our dangerous jungle. Different forces stimulate innovation, while others sabotage it. You have to know how the politics of innovation work to succeed in Red Monkey® Innovation Management.

Part III discusses the different types of management. 2D-organisations are managed by 2D-managers, while 3D-organisations are in need of 3D-managers. The difference between these two types of managers is so dramatically large, that we need to make a seismic shift in management style to create an organisation where innovation can develop organically. If organisations succeed in this, the Red Monkey® Innovation Process will start enabling these organisations to survive in the 3D-era.

The final part of our journey highlights the importance of culture innovation. It is impossible to transform a 2D-organisation by simply doing the same things better. The company culture has to change so dramatically that you have no option but to embrace creative entrepreneurship in the field of organisational development. Business innovation and culture innovation need to become equally important, if you want to achieve an innovative organisation in the 3D-era.

PART I

FROM THE 2D TO THE 3D-ERA.
CHAOTIC TIMES, COMPANIES ADRIFT...

1 Change course or sink

Introduction

Let me start this story with a picture. You might be surprised at first, because what you see is not a jungle, nor is it chaos. What you see is a sturdy barge calmly drifting on a smooth sea. The captain sets sail with the conviction that his ship is prepared to cross from the twentieth to the twenty-first century. Or, to be more exact, from the technological era to the era of information and innovation.

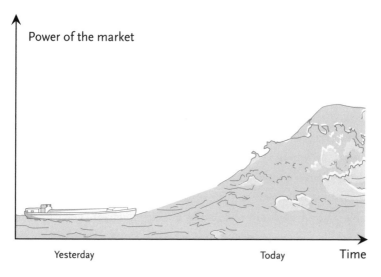

Figure 1 · *Organisations are facing turbulent times; but are they ready?*

The captain's mistakes become immediately clear: neither the ship nor the crew are ready for the ocean. The ship wasn't built to withstand such turbulent waters and the crew isn't trained for this new environment. They are unaware of the dangers and do not realise that storms at sea are a lot fiercer than the strong headwinds of inland waters. The high waves which the ship will have to endure are not like the choppy waters of a canal, when two ships pass each other or when one ship overtakes the other.

And there is another difficulty which the captain did not anticipate: the information that he and his crew receive while at sea is far more extensive and complex than when the ship was still in calm inland waters. This is an ocean of information, which constantly renews and grows: in these waters, other navigation skills are needed to prevent the ship from drifting aimlessly and eventually running aground.

"But what about that jungle?" you might ask. Patience! We will get to that in Part II. Before we can enter the world of the jungle and find our path towards change and innovation, we need to cross over to a new dimension. Or perhaps I should say to an extra dimension. We are going to make the transition from a two-dimensional environment – a canal with shores nearby to our left and right, where we can moor safely at any time – to a more dangerous three-dimensional world. Here, the shores are gone, the horizon is unknown and the disorienting currents are unpredictable. Calm waters are replaced by a whirling chaos. The captain's old skills and experience are useless here. To steer the barge safely towards the future, new currents have to be discovered and navigated, as the ocean beneath the ship gets wilder and wilder. No wonder a lot of managers and employees get seasick!

Old salts know the cure for seasickness: go on deck and focus on a fixed spot on the horizon. This simple comparison presents us with our first solution: management must articulate a challenging vision for the future that foresees trends and takes proper account of them, in order to provide the entire crew with a fixed spot on the horizon.

Unfortunately, the reality is often different. The managers are seasick on deck or they retreat to their cabins, hoping the storm will pass. Others try to weather the storm, giving useless, sometimes contradictory instructions that lead to even more stress and chaos. The old, calm balance has disappeared.

You might say: "Why do we have to cross the ocean in the first place? Why can't we just stay safely in port?" Let me start by showing you the various signs and omens which indicate that a storm is brewing. If you don't take these signs into account and you don't change your course – in short, if you don't muster the courage to cross that ocean – then you are lost.

The role of information in the 3D-era

In the introduction I pointed out that we are rapidly evolving from a two-dimensional world into a three-dimensional one; from 2D to 3D. This concept reappears later in the book. Through the allegory of ocean navigation, you now understand the nature of this dramatic change and you know that 'information' and 'innovation' are key words. They are responsible for the growing stress and chaos in organisations. The transition to the 3D-world can only happen when we fully realise the roles which information and innovation will play. They are absolutely critical to our chances of survival.

You can also view the flood of information that continually washes over us from a different perspective: this information flood is the critical fifth element for survival in this new world. Water, fire, air, earth – and now information – are all crucial for life.

Strictly speaking, we are "in our element" when we have sufficient oxygen to breathe, solid ground to stand on, water to drink and fire to warm ourselves. Given the above analogy, you might assume that information would also have a positive, soothing influence. Yet this does not appear to be the case. A lot of people consider the growing amount of information to be a threat. There is too much of it and nothing to control or stop it.

In the past, we learned to gather as much knowledge as possible about as many things as possible. This was the basic idea behind the Age of Enlightenment and the belief in *homo universalis*, the all-knowing man. Now we are beginning to realise that we can no longer master everything, not even in our own field of expertise. Nevertheless, we still have the same basic view on knowledge as before: if you study hard enough in your own chosen field, you will stay informed about everything. Complete control of all information was – and still is – the ultimate goal.

Only when we learn to breathe *information, at our own pace, will we fully understand its developmental power.*

Imagine how uncomfortable today's knowledge-freak must feel! How can he possibly handle the flow of information without drowning in it? The only answer to this problem is selectivity. If you fan the flames too high, your house will burn down. An athlete who does not control his breathing will soon be out of breath. You cannot survive in the information era, unless you breathe and filter information at your own pace, according to your own interests and passions. In short: you need to have the courage to select the right dose and the correct composition. Your intuition has to aid you in this task: that is the essence of success.

TECHNOLOGY AS AN INFORMATION CARRIER

If you lack oxygen, you will be put on a resuscitator. If you are thirsty, you drink. If you need information – and we assume that this need is permanent and insatiable – you must find streams of information where you can – selectively – quench your thirst.

Today, the most important source of information is the Internet and its related new media tools. In view of this fact, it is incomprehensible how few decision-makers are truly aware of the potential of the Internet. Even more astonishingly, many of them are young entrepreneurs and executives.

Unfortunately, the failure to assimilate these new tools and communication techniques may hurt decision-makers severely. It is not enough merely to be aware of their existence; they also have to be utilised fully, in order to limit your own vulnerability. Without the full utilisation of these modern communication technologies, development will be restricted or severely hampered. We need to keep a careful finger on the pulse.

If any single country ever succeeds in becoming the most innovative in the world, it will be because that country has dared to give the latent potential of its youth a chance. It is amazing how quickly our children can learn and, perhaps even more importantly, how quickly they learn from each other. By this, of course, I mean the Internet phenomenon: instant messaging, chat rooms, virtual gaming with virtual teams, forums, communities, personal websites and access to enormous amounts of information. The only investments needed to make all this possible are a PC and access to the world-wide web. Everything else, such as how to utilise this amazingly powerful combination, they are able to learn by themselves. By experimenting and by learning from each other they acquire skills that many adults cannot rival or even understand. And I am not just referring to technical expertise, but also to the social skills needed to communicate with others in a completely new environment. Children have a lot more access to information than their parents' generation and this is both new and unique. In the past, parents, teachers and employers always knew more than the young. It was the cornerstone of their power.

"Shut up and listen... you're too young to know." This mentality is deeply ingrained in our culture – and we need to get rid of it. Until now, we have always thought that knowledge is power – but it's not that straightforward anymore.

We can no longer compel obedience and discipline by simply nipping unwanted discussions in the bud. More than anything, our youth needs guidance and wisdom. How do you deal with this new environment? How do you use it to continually improve yourself with knowledge that is useful to you? But herein lies the problem: how do you guide someone in an environment which you yourself do not fully understand? Most adults consider the Internet to be a waste of time. At best, they want to use it to book a cheap flight. They look at it in much the same way as our ancestors looked at the first steam train, the first telephone or the first television. If we do not drastically change our approach, we will not only lose out in terms of economic innovation, but will also miss opportunities for social and educational improvement.

Everything starts with education. However, teachers are unskilled and reluctant users of the new media. They still swear by an educational model based on the one-sided introduction of new subject material. This must change. What we need is less 'subject material' and a more effective learning process, a process which gives the teacher more time to find a new balance between the old and the new learning models, with the help of his students. This requires a willingness to learn and to make mistakes. It is a process in which the teacher and the students are on the same level. The teacher no longer gets his 'directing' power from his knowledge, but rather from the respect he commands as a coach and facilitator. This exact same method must also be applied in the economic sector and in our companies. Managers will have to deal with young employees who know more and learn faster than they do. Power will no longer be based on expertise, but on vision, open mindedness and enthusiasm. Keep this in mind while you read this book.

You are still not convinced? Think about this: thanks to the Internet, people from all around the world can now get in touch with each other at the touch of a button. Such contact existed in the past but to a much lesser degree. Innovative insights and ideas were spread at conventions, colloquia and in specialist magazines, dissertations and other publications.

Nowadays, it is different and faster – a lot faster. Thanks to Internet forums, web conferences and other means, information can be transferred and 'enriched' instantly. If you do not participate in this process, you will be left hopelessly behind. More often than not, this process of rapid information transfer happens outside the organisation. Moreover, it is almost totally undirected by management, even though it constantly results in new services and products. It is "an invasion of innovation".

Another difficulty which increases the information chaos is the fact that the information revolution is no longer driven solely by "the West". There are other players in the game: from Asia and South America, from Eastern Europe and – don't be surprised in the not too distant future – from Africa as well. That means that innovation does not always have a 'western' slant to it. Once again, our barge is being assailed by a gigantic wave. Do you remember how difficult it was to overcome the Japanese wave in the late 20th century? What we are facing now is even more colossal. Of course, we could throw up larger embankments: create a protected market, concentrate primarily on national interests and bury our heads in the sand. However, I very much doubt whether these precautions would prevent the river banks from bursting.

The main problem is that we simply do no see the danger. We think that competition only exists between rich and poor regions and that this competition is essentially about wages. However, there is a lot of direct competition between low-wage countries as well and it is all related to the provision of innovative services and products. High-wage countries with little power to innovate should be very concerned about the consequences of this new battle. If wages do not go down, high-wage countries can only survive by drastically increasing their own innovative power.

Chaos leads to balance

Chaos provides balance. This sounds like a paradox, but if you are acquainted with system thinking, it actually makes sense. No matter how absurd the now famous image of the hurricane-causing butterfly might be, there is a kernel of truth in it. A tidal wave recedes and leaves behind destruction in its wake, but this gives us the opportunity to rebuild the things that have been washed away – and this rebuilding can sometimes lead to better results than before.

Of course, I do not want this to happen to your particular organisation. The realisation that a breech in our protective dykes is inevitable, coupled with the fact that chaos always leads to a new balance, will provide you with the opportunity to prevent the disaster before it ever happens.

The growing tidal wave of information spreading across the globe is causing an enormous increase in the rate of change. All these changes lead to trends, trends which also have a mutual influence on each other. The flat, controlled environment in which our barge once existed has been transformed into a chaotically changing ocean in just ten years. This new environment appears to be without balance. But this is not the case. In fact, there are several trends or patterns influencing one another in a structured manner within this chaos – and it is this combination which determines the behaviour of chaos. In turn, this behaviour determines what will happen to the world, to markets, to societies, to organisations, to your company and – eventually – to all of us.

Consequently, the key to success lies in accepting and embracing chaos as a fact. By no longer resisting chaos with short-sighted, short-term solutions but by using it and by integrating it into all the various aspects of an organisation, we can take an enormous step towards creating an organisation that can withstand the harsh realities of a 3D-world.

Conclusion: wake up!

Identifying trends is the first condition for every organisation to make the safe transition from the two-dimensional to the three-dimensional world. If this does not happen, the organisation will become a plaything of the ocean, tossed by the turbulent waves, swamped by the changing powers of others.

The captain of a sea-worthy organisation is consciously looking for the right winds and currents, so that he can not only guide his ship on a safe route, but also generate the highest possible speed. The captain who fails to do this and who does not involve his crew in plotting the new course will end up with an out-of-control vessel, which will run aground sooner or later.

At a time when organisations require radical changes in order to survive, management frequently neglects its obligation to act. This results in the failure of most change processes. Sadly, this is nothing new. In 1992, Schieman said: "One of the most important challenges of companies is staying ahead of quick changes in the market. Most managers know this but actually doing something about it is very difficult. Less than 50% of changing projects succeed."

Patricia A. McLagan (*Training & Development Magazine*, November 2002) says that the success rates of deliberate change programmes are not high: "67 percent of total quality management initiatives end with no results after two years." So it is clear: a seasick management that doesn't see the real trends and doesn't develop a solid vision of the future for – and with – their crew will not succeed in making the necessary changes to keep the ship seaworthy.

Organisations in trouble do not have too few crew members
It is simply that the crew does not perform.

Recently, I came across a summary of the Gallup Organisation's Employee Engagement Index Survey for 2002. The results of this research, assessing the commitment of employees, were painful. At a time when everyone's contribution is necessary to assist the sorely needed process of change, the majority of the crew is failing in its duty. Only twenty percent of employees feel actively involved in the organisation's well-being. Sixty percent are neutral. Twenty percent are actively disengaged and do all in their power to boycott change processes.

Captains who do not want their ship to run aground have a lot of work to do. Wake up! Now!

2 Transition to the 3D-era

Introduction

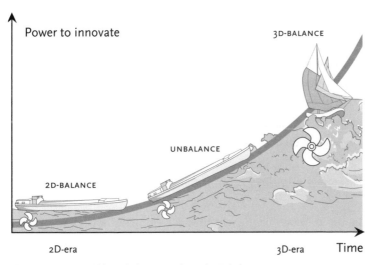

Figure 2 · *From a stable 2D-balance to a dynamic 3D-balance*

In chapter 1, I introduced the terms '2D' (two-dimensional) and '3D' (three-dimensional) to indicate how the world in which we (and our companies) function is evolving. The idea was strengthened with a metaphor: the unprepared barge that goes out to sea.

In this chapter, I will explain that the transition from the 2D-era to the 3D-era will also have consequences for the current balance of the business world. It is important to know that the switch from

2D to 3D will not happen without a struggle. If you sail from a river towards the sea, you must first cross the inshore breakers before reaching open water. And even then, the first storms will trouble your ship consideralby, because it is simply not prepared.

There will be an old 2D and a new 3D-balance, as shown in figure 2. Later in the book, you will read how 2D differs from 3D. You will also learn that the 3D-balance will never be firm and stable, and that you and your team members will have to go to great lengths to maintain your balance. Always keep in mind that it is impossible to pass unscathed from one balance to the other, because finding your 3D-balance is inevitably an arduous search process. It is like learning to ride a bike all over again, but this time without training wheels. Let this be a warning for those who tend to give up easily.

From a two-dimensional balance…

In the previous century, running a company was characterised by clear controllable parameters. Organisations moved horizontally, straight ahead, two-dimensionally. This reassuring balance was supported by logical, provable calculations, which formed the basis for clear-cut decisions.

Growth and evolution followed steady, unquestioned patterns. Continuous improvement was enough to maintain the plotted course. Or to put it in management terms: return on investment was guaranteed. In fact, it was all very simple: if ROI wasn't guaranteed, if uncertainty arose, then the ship was brought about and started to cruise in a different direction. As a result, investment would decline or cease altogether.. Later, you will understand that this is one of the biggest differences with a three-dimensional organisation.

The captains and crews of these late 20th century ships can be best described as 'spreadsheet-managers'. Anyone who could use spreadsheet-macros was the absolute best, the bee's knees. Why? Because he was capable of calculating the results of the anticipated improvements ahead of time, within variable parameters. In short, he limited risks and achieved results.

Companies increasingly needed this kind of talented manager. Large organisations were looking for a fleet of barges to replace their one big super tanker. It became clear that it was difficult to steer a super tanker through narrow channels, particularly when the company's course meandered from left to right. It was too cumbersome to react quickly to the increasing fluctuations of the market. The single large spreadsheet which supervised everything was replaced by a hierarchy of smaller spreadsheets.

The manager held absolute sway over his ship: choosing the direction, solving problems, giving advice and guiding employees through their daily activities. It was his responsibility. It was also the correct management style at a time when the business environment was flat. The 2D-balance.

... through turbulent waters...

How can you possibly keep your organisation afloat in today's modern world, if you do not constantly anticipate – or even go consciously in search of – new external influences? If you do not see the waves of change approaching, you will be swept off the bridge. This is exactly what is happening today. Running away from risks is no longer an option. We are already too far out at sea. Safe harbours are nowhere to be found and there is no way back.

The predictable, horizontal balance has been replaced by a gigantic 360 degree horizon. The navigational maps that you have been using until now are worthless and the spreadsheet-predictions often turn out to be wrong, so that they need to be adjusted regularly. Consequently, the ship needs to change direction more often. The crew is not comfortable with this and they start to wonder if the captain still knows where he is heading. Every new change – another reorganisation, another restructuring – burns precious energy and wears down morale.

... to a new three-dimensional balance

Is there nothing you can do to regain control of the ship? Of course there is! New trends appear: waves push you forward and, if you make good use of them, they can even provide you with an alternative source of power for your ship.

Today's captain no longer stares blindly at his maps; instead, he constantly searches the horizon for suitable waves and for the right wind. He rapidly transforms his ship from a slow, fragile barge into a fast, manoeuvrable motor-sailboat, which gets part of its energy from the wind and part from the waves. Vision and passion are the tools he now uses to reach his destination! But above all, he uses his rediscovered intuition: the intuition to make the right decisions with insufficient information. Or, as Albert Einstein once said, "The intuitive mind is a sacred gift and the rational mind is a faithful servant. We have created a society that honours the servant and has forgotten the gift."

If trends are waves, then it is vision which allows you to ride tho-
se waves.

The result is a new organisation, an organisation that can move effortlessly through the three-dimensional space. Thanks to intuition, there will be calm in the chaos. The balance is restored, the ship is steady again and the crew is reassured. But the acquired 3D-balance only remains stable as long as your company's intuition is sound. Don't get overconfident and don't ever let routine replace intuition. If you do, the ship could easily capsize once more...

In conclusion: new crew wanted!

Organisations which were built like 2D-barges and which were once market leaders are now facing a dramatic dilemma.

Because many managers feel unwell on the uncertain waves of the dynamic 3D-balance, they will attempt to keep the sea 'flat', trying to get as much solid surface underneath their feet as possible. An entire generation of managers and employees will find it hard to leave the predictable 2D-balance, unwilling to become masters in the world of the unpredictable 3D-balance. They will simply not be able to make the leap.

This poses a painful question for the organisation: will you educate and retrain the old crew, so they can stay on board when you sail into the 3D-ocean? Or will you replace them with a completely new crew, one which has no problem facing the challenges of the 3D-balance?

This latter type of new manager and employee already exists! They feel comfortable in the chaotic 3D-environment. They are thrilled – not frightened – that there is so much information available to them. With their team, they somehow manage to find a way through the turbulent market. This new generation of employees and managers is starting to manifest itself and they will give shape to tomorrow's organisations. Just like the captains of the old sailboats, they do not feel at ease on land. They need movement, unpredictability and adventure. They stay on their feet, no matter how much they have to struggle for balance. But eventually they will find this balance – their 3D-balance – and they will succeed, thanks to their passion for everything that is new.

An organisation with a challenging vision on organisational development should start looking actively for this new type of manager today! These are the people who can provide the extra oxygen needed for the effective makeover of an organisation.

3 What is innovation?

Introduction

Before we finally enter the jungle of your organisation, we need to make one more thing absolutely clear. If you have read this far, you might be a little confused. You might even be asking yourself: "Hasn't innovation always been with us? Isn't mankind's entire history marked by inventions, new insights, evolutions and revolutions?"

You are undoubtedly correct, but at the same time you must also admit that many inventions were discovered by accident – or, at least, not on purpose. You will also understand that certain evolutions were simply adaptations of existing situations and that they were not actual goals in themselves. When I talk about 'innovation' in this book, I mean a never-ending, active renewing process inside the company or organisation. This renewal process is the actual goal in itself. To clarify this point, let us examine the concept of 'innovation' more closely. Figure 3 will help to explain.

It is easy to reduce the word 'innovation' to its core meaning: the introduction of something new. This definition might be clear to everyone but putting it into practice is an entirely different matter. Achieving an innovative organisation is a lot more difficult and complex than it may seem.

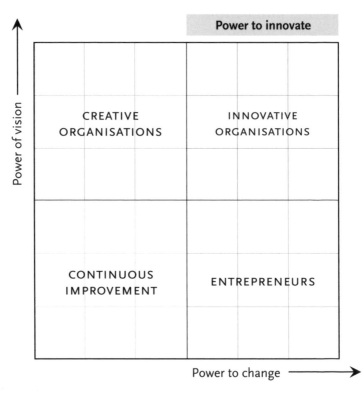

Figure 3 · *Innovation is a collaboration between the power of vision and the power to change*

Figure 3 represents innovation as a combination of two important factors: power of vision and the power to change. We might characterise current innovation, as it is regarded in most of today's organisations, as being '2D-innovation', analogous with the idea of the 2D-era and the 2D-balance. Today's innovation could easily be described as two-dimensional: flat and horizontal. It is predictable and the return on investment is visible.

FROM THE 2D TO THE 3D-ERA

However, the innovation of the new 3D-era has a different characteristic. It is, by definition, unpredictable, because it is not simply the continuation of something which is already happening. The greater the power of vision and the power to change, the more powerful 3D-innovation becomes. As a result, this increases the likely rate of success.

Continuous improvement in the 2D-era

Innovation in the old 2D-balance happened in a controlled and predictable manner, tailored to the market and primarily focused on company processes, product upgrades and service enhancements. Today, the majority of entrepreneurs still think in these terms. In the 2D-era, innovation is the answer to a visible need. Eventually, it results in the concept of 'continuous improvement' or 'kaizen' (Japanese for "improving by change", first used in a management context by the American Frederick Winslow Taylor). In the previous century this idea was formalised in processes like the well-known ISO-9000 and EFQM labels.

> *ISO-9000 and EFQMK have entrenched organisations in the 2D-era. This was never the intention of ISO-9000 and EFQM.*

The 'power of vision' (see figure 3) in these processes is limited to seeing the possibilities for change. The results of the subsequent changes are immediately visible and the 'power to change' is nothing more than the straightforward investment in change processes, as long as the return on investment is immediately calculable. In short, creativity is being used to search for new, concrete results. Late 20th century decision-makers liked this, because every change remained controllable and calculable: a necessity in the 2D-era, when everything revolved around certainty. The word 'risk' is nowhere to be found in their dictionary.

As I have already said, the 2D-era is over. This exposes a conflict that drives many company leaders to desperation. How can they bridge the gap between the 2D and the 3D-era; 2D and 3D-balance; 2D and 3D-innovation? How can an organisation, built on the safe ground of continuous improvement, survive in the 3D-era, where everything is uncertain and where balance is seemingly absent?

Real innovation starts in the 3D-era

To innovate successfully in this new era, a radical break with the past is essential. This requires an enormous mental effort from managers and CEO's alike. In particular, as we have already learned, intuition will slowly regain its rightful place in the business world.

Those who were born and raised in the 2D-era will find this very hard to swallow. All certainty is gone. To innovate nowadays, the organisation must break with everything it knew and with everything it used to do. Processes, products and services from the past *belong* in the past. Investment in 'something new' is now a necessity, even though immediate return on investment is not guaranteed. From now on, creativity is no longer searching for concrete results, but for something that does not yet exist.

Creativity and business are fused together into a process of creative entrepreneurship, in which the ability to make correct decisions with limited information (and a lot of intuition!) is of the utmost importance.

> *In the 3D-era, creative people are always looking for entrepreneurs and entrepreneurs are always looking for creative people. Innovation is what happens when they meet.*

As a result, the power of vision will henceforth also include the recognition, the acceptance and even the prediction of trends. This makes it possible to outline an intuitive course for the organisation in the new environment.

Consequently, the power to change will mean 'investing in the realisation of an intuitive vision'. It will be 'instinctively' clear that a return on investment is possible, but not guaranteed.

Consensus versus conflict

The difference between real innovation and continuous improvement is now evident. Nevertheless, some questions do arise and require answers. Innovation, as any entrepreneur knows, is not without risk. Can today's organisations still cope with a growing multiplicity of risks? Yes, but in the future, guts and courage will be as important as intuition and creativity in the business world.

After all, innovation can only succeed if management is willing to give it a chance. Making room for creative business requires cultural changes in the organisation. (This will be dealt with in Part II of this book). Top managers in an innovative 3D-environment concentrate primarily on offering security to a new generation of managers and employees who are willing to set an example – by taking risks.

This requires managers to abandon the safety of the 'consensus model' and deploy a 'conflict model' instead. Companies cannot evolve from 2D to 3D-organisations within a framework of consensus and democracy: the power of 2D-managers and employees would remain too great. After all, the cautious 2D-ers are always in the majority. If ten sharks and one dolphin have a vote on who will be eaten, the answer is obvious: the dolphin loses.

This has been happening for years and will still happen during the first transitional phase in 2D-organisations. Those who propose a risky or confrontational idea will be voted down. Quite often these brave men and women will even be forced to leave the ship, deciding to resign with honour before the axe falls. And as these adventurers lower a lifeboat to safety, they may look back with sadness at the rusty ship that they unsuccessfully tried to steer to another course.

> *Continuous improvement in the 2D-era is a consensus model.*
> *Continuous innovation in the 3D-era is a conflict model.*

This creates an obvious dilemma? How will you be able to convince the cautious majority in a 2D-organisation to transform into a 3D-organisation? You will discover the answers to this question in Part II.

Conclusion: the jungle beckons

The previous paragraphs might have confused you. Are improvement and innovation the opposite of one another? No, of course, they are not. Continuous improvement remains a necessity for every organisation – but by itself, it is no longer sufficient.

It is equally ridiculous to think that the idea of gradual improvement is a thing of the past and that from now on investment should only be made with the aim of complete renewal and total innovation. Putting your ship on a new course does not mean you that have to dismantle it completely!

Having said that, if you only continue to use the same old methods as before, you might as well have dismantled it! The importance of real innovation will grow in the years ahead and it will take its rightful place beside improvement. Intuition and creative business will become key concepts. Only organisations which change their 2D-culture into a 3D-culture will be able to survive. The new captain of the future will not be someone who tries to steer the course on his own, but rather someone who is aided by the initiatives and ingenuity of his crew. This captain will have a vision and will be capable of altering the ship's course at any given moment. He will constantly urge his crew to come up with creative new ideas which deviate from the planned course, in the hope of catching a better wind. Naturally, the risk of making a mistake is ever present. But with so much creativity on board, a mistake on a 3D-ship will never be as serious as a mistake on a 2D-ship, with its lonely captain manning the bridge.

Nevertheless, it is clear that the level of risk will be a step too far for many, content as they are with their 2D-balance. To prevent themselves from losing their footing, they will resist the 3D-era with all the strength they can muster. They are afraid, but they cannot – and must not – be allowed to succeed.

It is time for us to leave the "company as a ship" metaphor and go ashore. We are now standing at the edge of a jungle, the place where the transition from 2D to 3D commences. In other words, we are standing at the edge of your organisation...

PART II

....

AN ANSWER TO THE 3D CHALLENGE:
RED MONKEY® POLITICS

4 A challenging idea appears in the jungle

Introduction

If you want to prepare your organisation to face the challenges of the information and innovation age, you must understand that the time for change is now. To become as well prepared as you possibly can be, you need to combine two qualities: vision and intuition. These need to be supported by creativity and entrepreneurship.

This might look easy to accomplish, but it is not (as was indicated at the end of chapter 3). The difficulty of transforming an existing, non-innovative 2D-organisation into a flexible 3D-organisation, where innovation has free rein, should not be underestimated. Above all, the existing organisational structure will not allow this to happen and it will not stand aside without a struggle.

Let me use another analogy. Imagine that a Red Monkey appears from nowhere in the middle of the jungle. No one has ever seen an animal like this before. How do the other monkeys react? And the other animals? The poor little Red Monkey will be killed immediately, because it disturbs the ruling order and challenges the existing system and its certainties. Most creative ideas meet the same fate in a 2D-organisation: they are executed without mercy.

It is almost contradictory to say that something innovative can be produced from something non-innovative. Or to put it another way: that a non-innovative organisation 'somehow' has to find the innovative skills to evolve into an innovative organisation. The stability of a 2D-organisation obstructs this evolution: it is so strong that culture change is almost impossible.

So should you give up hope? Not at all, because in this chapter you will learn how you can build up a 3D-organisation from a 2D-organisation. All you need is Red Monkey Politics.

The origin of a new species

Joel Baker (Chesapeake Biological Laboratory, University of Maryland) has helped us to understand why Red Monkeys fail to survive in the heart of the jungle. To explain this, he made the challenging statement that biodiversity does not originate in the heart of the rainforest. According to Baker, most radical change processes take place at the edge of the forest, where the jungle meets another ecosystem, such as the sea. Here both systems are able to pollinate one another. Scientific research confirms Baker's claim.

Even so, until recently biologists were convinced that biodiversity evolved from the centre to the edge of the forest and not the other way around. Why? Simply because the heart of the forest was the place where the greatest degree of biodiversity could be found.

If we put this theory into the context of organisational change, you will immediately understand the essence of this book. Organisations still think that change can only start at the heart of the organisation. This is the place where many of the plans for change are conceived and implemented ... only to be immediately shot down or sabotaged.

Real change does not start at the centre of the organisation. It slowly permeates the organisation from its borders. How did the Red Monkey we have just encountered actually enter the jungle? Where did it come from? To explain this further, I will use the metaphor of the Red Monkey and its origins, basing my explanation on Baker's hypothesis.

Imagine a brown monkey from the jungle exploring the edge of the forest near the coast. There it meets a red fish. In the course of their conversation, they happen upon a new idea: a Red Monkey. Well, it is the same in organisations: you meet people who are consciously looking for new ideas along the borders with other ecosystems. I call these people Red Monkey Breeders. They embrace trends, information, technology, innovation and chaos. Time and time again, they create ideas that confront or threaten the existing order. They cut across the usual thinking patterns of the organisation and its people.

The Red Monkey Breeder is so enthusiastic about his new discovery that he runs off into the jungle with his innovative idea – the Red Monkey – and shows it to everyone. For him it is a matter of the utmost importance to bring it to the centre of the jungle as quickly as possible. He is enthusiastic about his new idea, his new baby. It might be a possible solution to a problem, a drastic improvement, a clever new approach, a possible new product or service – or even a vacuum cleaner without a bag! James Dyson scoured Great Britain and Europe for two years to find investors for his new product. The multinationals hesitated, because they feared that the market for vacuum bags, which generates an annual profit of £100,000,000, would collapse. Eventually someone believed in the product and the vacuum cleaner without a bag became a huge commercial success.

Not all Red Monkey Breeders are as lucky as Dyson – although all of them are probably as proud of their inventions and think that everyone will share in their excitement and enthusiasm. But this is part of the problem: in their euphoria they lose sight of the Red Monkey Hunter. They don't see the danger coming, until it's already too late. And then the inevitable happens.

> *What is a Red Monkey?*
> *A Red Monkey is a confrontational idea which disturbs the balance in people, teams and organisations. It is an idea that challenges established values and processes and thus generates both considerable support and resistance: it is therefore an opportunity for some and a threat to others. Innovation is the result of a Red Monkey which has survived the initial conflict between these two opposing points of view.*

Unfortunately, this means that in most cases the Red Monkey is killed in infancy. The idea conveyed by the Red Monkey Breeder is so disturbing, so confrontational and so likely to upset the existing order that managers and employees with powerful egos will destroy it immediately. The majority of people in organisations even enjoy hunting down and slaying these defenceless, some-times still embryonic ideas. They are the Red Monkey Hunters.

This is often the fate of challenging ideas in 2D-organisations. They die the minute they are conceived. It is an illusion to suppose that this internal Red Monkey hunt will ever stop. Nevertheless, it is important to realise that in our current era this hunt will not only kill Red Monkeys: it will eventually kill the hunting organisations as well.

The inevitable condition: open innovation

If your organisation's chance of survival does indeed depend on the number of challenging new ideas it can generate, you must immediately put all your energy into the creation of as many Red Monkeys as possible. This is another tough pill to swallow, but there is a useful fertilisation technique to help you accomplish this: open innovation.

Instead of looking for sources of innovation within your own organisation, you should get in touch with other ecosystems, pref-erably organisations from completely different sectors: profit, non-profit, social profit, industry, services, large, small...

Real change does not start at the heart of an organisation; it per-meates the organisation from its borders.

Most new ideas are born from new contacts and new networks; ideas that simply *could not* be invented by people who remained within their own ecosystem. These inspirational external inputs can lead to improvement or innovation inside the company, or sometimes to a completely new concept which different companies and organisations can then further develop together.

Here are some new concepts for the world of organisational development:

OPEN INNOVATION: the active stimulation of networking between organisations, suppliers and customers, with the aim of innovating more quickly. The organisation 'opens' itself to others.

DIVERSITY IN ACTION: the uniting of as many diversities (ecosystems) as possible, in order to innovate more quickly. The most innovative regions in the world derive their creative power from their diverse cultures.

IN-COMPANY OPEN INNOVATION: actively stimulating innovation processes *inside* the organisation and between different departments. You might be surprised, but most organisations which claim to cherish open innovation and cooperation with others do not manage to run their own internal open innovation process. You probably know several examples where business units or branches flatly refuse to learn from one another. All too often, the knowledge and experience which is already present in-house remains unused elsewhere within the organisation. In other words, if open innovation is to succeed, it has to resonate *inside* the organisation, as well as on the outside.

Open innovation requires transparency and honesty. It wakes up both the organisation and its employees. It opens a window to let in the outside world. For this reason, open innovation also meets with a lot of resistance. It's like being forced to wake up. By consciously looking for contact with the outside world, you bring an alarm clock into the organisation. This alarm clock rouses people from a state we call 'unconsciously incompetent'. This is the most blissful condition a human being can possibly be in: you don't know that you don't know. Or to put it another way: you think you know everything, that you are invincible. Everyone wants to feel this way. We cover ourselves with a blanket of invincibility and immortality. "We are already innovative enough." "We do everything better than the others." "We have already been doing that for years". These are the phrases that keep the door closed for open innovation.

Too many people have developed an unwitting aversion to change. They sleep without knowing it and when they hear the alarm go off, they smash it to pieces. However, they still like to proclaim that they are 'the best', preferably at expensive conferences with dressed-up 'best practices'. It is important not to confuse this arrogant conduct with open innovation.

Open innovation is opening yourself up to the ideas and suggestions of others. Open innovation also requires a particular kind of social behaviour. People from different organisations will only share information if they feel that there is a 'connection'. Empathy for others, listening actively, respect and equality are some of the necessary keywords, if open innovation is to have a chance of success.

Conclusion: it's open innovation or death!

Jungles are actually very stable systems. They might seem chaotic, because of their biological diversity, but in essence a jungle is an interplay of balanced processes. Nature provides natural balance. Elements which disturb that balance are literally and figuratively devoured.

Today, organisations can no longer afford the luxury of maintaining the status quo, the old ruling order. To survive in the information and innovation era, a tidal wave of innovative ideas is called for, in order to support the organisation's flexibility, so that it can surf on each and every wave of change.

For this reason, it is essential to disturb the natural balance within organisations. To achieve this? You have to make sure that challenging new ideas are not immediately killed off. Those who actively search for and introduce these new ideas are the Red Monkey Breeders. Their breeding grounds are not found at the heart of the organisation, but at its edge, where they keep in close contact with Red Monkey Breeders from other organisations. By supporting these new ideas and preventing them from dying in their embryonic stages, you are promoting open innovation: stimulating contact with people from other sectors.

But beware: the majority of managers and employees have a built-in defence mechanism. These are the Red Monkey Hunters. Such people must change their hostile behaviour, by allowing new ideas to flood their thinking. They need to open their eyes, ears and mind to innovation. If this does not happen, your plans for a 3D-organisation will remain nothing more than a Utopian dream.

5 Profile of a Red Monkey® Hunter

Introduction

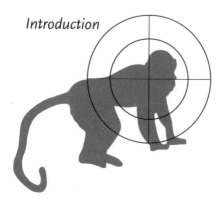

It should by now be obvious where the greatest threat to an organisation resides, as it tries to cross over from the 2D-era to the 3D-era. Most employees still have a 2D-attitude and will do all that they can to jeopardise the crossing. But cross over you must, if you want to remain successful. This means that you need to understand the profile of the 2D-people in your organisation

There is no reason to panic. These employees – or at least quite a number of them – can be 'rescued' and can play a part in the new 3D-organisation. But to take them that far, you must first get inside the mind of these enemies of the Red Monkeys.

You will learn that Red Monkey Hunters act in subtle ways. Essentially, they do nothing wrong and they won't be caught breaking the rules. They are not revolutionary, nor do they incite revolutions in others. So how do they kill Red Monkeys time and time again?

What is their motivation? If you understand this, you (and they) will be able to overcome their resistance.

Searching for a stable balance

2D and 3D-organisations are both looking for balance, but there is a major difference between the equilibrium they seek. 3D-balance is dynamic. It must be continually rediscovered. It's like walking on a high-wire; it is difficult, but those who can pull it off deserve to be applauded.

By comparison, 2D-balance is a lot safer. It keeps your feet firmly on the deck and uses a safety rope, so that you can't fall overboard, not even when a storm gathers. Red Monkey Hunters are always looking for this 2D kind of balance. They are aided by the fact that most of today's organisational systems are run in such a way that they respect safety and stability above all else. The moment something in the system becomes 'chaotic', the necessary processes are immediately set in motion to repair the balance. As a result, nothing changes.

Compare this to life in the jungle. If a particular species – insects, for example – increases dramatically in number, the number of predators will automatically increase as well. When the hunted species decreases, the system regulates itself again. I was once taught that there are never more fish in a pond than there is food. If you feed them more, they'll breed like ... rabbits! If you don't feed them at all, their number will decrease. It is very difficult to disturb this kind of system, but maintaining it is a piece of cake. This is the problem faced by Red Monkeys.

An organisation in the 2D-era strives for absolute stability. It's rather like the thermostat in a house, which keeps the temperature at a constant level without anyone noticing. Spreadsheets and related processes are the ideal tools for 2D-managers and employees to use, in order to keep this balance in place. This kind of organisation is like a heavy slab of concrete, immune to even the tiniest crack. Only processes which reinforce this monolithic block have any chance of survival.

> *Improvement processes are the mortar of 2D-organisation. They harden the organisational culture. This was fast enough for the 2D-era, but is far too slow for the 3D-era.*

Perhaps this explains the success of ISO 9000 and EFQM. These norms solidify the procedures and rules in an organisation – like reinforced concrete – thereby ensuring that the organisation can only follow the path of constant (and usually slow) improvement. The resulting balance is so strong that the numerous Red Monkey Hunters – who have ensconced themselves in all the hierarchical layers of the organisation – can eliminate every unsettling, innovative Red Monkey with a single shot.

It must be obvious that this 'procedural cement' makes it almost impossible to transform a 2D-organisation into a 3D-organisation. After all, in this 2D-system modernisation and change need to stay within predictable limits. The organisation must continue to operate like it has always operated. Any initiative which might possibly cause instability is neutralised. This happens so spontaneously that employees and managers hardly even notice it anymore: they are so used to it. This challenging thought also explains why

AN ANSWER TO THE 3D CHALLENGE: RED MONKEY® POLITICS

organisations, companies and even educational institutions have so many problems adapting to a rapidly changing world. The traditional thinking pattern of continuous improvement removes any space for innovation and change.

In this self-regulating business ecosystem, the Red Monkey Hunters are the dominant species. But before you can start diminishing their numbers – and perhaps even converting some of them to Red Monkey Breeders – you need to be able to recognise them. You need to understand the methods they use in their self-appointed mission to stabilise the organisation.

How can you recognize the Red Monkey® Hunter?

In chapter 6, I will clarify the relationship between the different groups that co-exist inside an organisation. Briefly summarised, these groups are: creators, pioneers, followers and settlers. For now, you only need to know that the settler group forms the core of the Red Monkey Hunter community.

This should come as no surprise. The word 'settler' contains the idea of 'stable balance'. The Red Monkey Hunters are those employees within your organisation who pass judgement on every change which might pose a threat to their stable life. Some of their typical comments are:

- This will never work.
- We've already tried that.
- Here we go again.
- We've only just changed everything.

- What's the guarantee that this will be better?
- We've been doing it like this for a hundred years. Why change now?
- We'll have to work even harder.
- This will cause total chaos and anarchy.
- I won't be responsible if it goes wrong.
- This has never succeeded anywhere.
- You still believe in fairytales.
- We're too old to go along with this.
- You can't keep changing all the time.

These are not the comments of people who are concerned about the wellbeing of your organisation. On the contrary: they are the comments of people who only think about themselves. Here are some examples of possible personal motives for this selfishness.

I DON'T UNDERSTAND IT, BUT I WON'T SHOW IT

A lot of managers in organisations still don't understand the Internet. Their aversion to using web-controlled communication tools is a good example of this lack of understanding. How many companies take the Instant Messaging phenomenon seriously? How many companies control the Internet usage of their employees? The main argument against the use of these tools is a 'belief' that the employees will no longer concentrate on their work and will spend all their time telling each other jokes via Instant Messaging or surfing the Internet for amusement. The same argument is also used to target Internet forums and communities. There are countless communities on the Internet today and they provide rich channels for finding and exchanging information at high speed (in both national and international contexts). How many innovative ideas pass by unnoticed, simply because this resource is not being exploited properly by the organisation's managers? Red Monkey Hunters simply do not understand the potential of the Internet: (de)motivated by this ignorance, they will sink any initiative which attempts to open up these channels.

Red Monkey Hunters don't understand new ideas and reject them because they don't want to reveal their own lack of knowledge.

MY PERSONAL STATUS IS IN DANGER, SO I DON'T EVEN WANT TO TALK ABOUT IT

Hierarchical and technical ladders make it possible for people to reach a certain position – and acquire a certain degree of status – within the organisation. These hierarchies create great resistance to proposed changes which threaten to redefine the organisational structure. What is needed is a transformation from a line organisation into a matrix organisation ... and, even further, into a network organisation. Current management resists these changes, because their own corporate future is threatened.

THE LADDER COLLAPSES

It's not easy getting older in a knowledge economy. Things used to be different. Studying hard, obtaining the right degree and having the right connections (via family or friends) was usually sufficient to guarantee a successful career. Most of the time it wasn't even a career, just a ladder of progression. You started on the bottom rung and you gradually made your way the top, gaining more power and more prestige as you climbed.

This type of hierarchical ladder is a strange thing. You can only go up... or stay where you are. You can't go down. This is mentally impossible. If you are forced to take a step downwards, the humiliation and loss of prestige is so painful that it is probably better to look for a new job.

Every day, it is becoming more evident that this 'ladder' principle only works in environments which rarely change. In this kind of organisation 'old-fashioned' people desperately cling to the ladder, even though they have no significant positive impact on company results – often quite the reverse. In quickly changing markets, hierarchical ladders will lead to the decline and eventual death of your organisation. There is too little space for quick, intuitive renewal. The organisation is simply too slow.

Perhaps it is better to push the ladder down to the ground – with or without the people on it. Maybe instead we should start to think about a podium: a management podium and an expert podium. In sport, people who have the necessary talent and who train hard enough will eventually win their place on the podium. A lack of talent or training will usually exclude you from it. This metaphor gives us a dynamic which can stimulate employees, thereby influencing the positive development of organisations.

Athletes know how this system works and they mentally prepare themselves for the moment when talent and training are no longer sufficient to allow them to excel in their sport. They know that one day they will have to look for another source of income. Sometimes they have a talent as a coach or trainer, so that they can climb the podium in a different way: this time not as a competitor, but as the guide of their successor. This natural circle ensures continuous innovation in sport. It encourages people to evolve into new roles which provide new meaning and further development. It leads to greater personal fulfilment and a new balance between the older 'coaching' generation and the 'innovative' younger generation.

How long will it take before HR-managers and CEOS with a more creative and entrepreneurial approach, realise the economic stupidity of hierarchical ladders and have the pioneering courage to explore the path to the podium? This new mental model can smooth out the road which leads to the new kind of learning organisation we need. This is an example of possible cultural innovation – a subject we will deal with further in Part IV.

I STAND BY MY IDEAS
AND CAN'T ADMIT THAT THEY ARE OUTDATED

Nowadays, changes happen at a very rapid rate. Sometimes it is better to stop what you are currently doing and start all over again with a new idea. This, however, is often a bridge too far for many managers and employees. They keep defending 'their' project, even when there is no longer any rational reason to do so. This means that processes which worked well in the 2D-era are continually developed and defended. As a result, new and better ideas get no chance at all.

The motives detailed above are more or less 'defendable', because the Red Monkey Hunter is genuinely convinced that they are acting in the organisation's best interests. This cannot be said for the next three arguments, where clearly the personal safety of the Red Monkey Hunter is the most important issue at stake.

I NO LONGER HAVE POTENTIAL FOR THE FUTURE, SO I WILL DEFEND THE OLD WAYS

Many managers and experts know full well that new technologies can lead to better and faster solutions, but still persist in defending older technologies. Their motivation is not rational; it is personal. They are thoroughly acquainted with the old technology and are afraid that they will not be able to master the new technology. They assume that that other people (read: younger people) will outdo them when it comes to making the transition.

I AM THE OLDEST, AND SO IT IS MY TURN

To many experts and managers, it is unthinkable that someone younger could actually be better then them, let alone that he (or she) could be their boss! Nevertheless, young people are generally better acquainted with new technologies and they also have management capability. Most of the time, resistance to youth in organisations is purely emotional. The fear of losing prestige – both inside and outside the organisation – is enough to provoke opposition.

Once upon a time, a hunter came home from the hunt and gave his spear to his son. He told him: "Son, it is your turn to hunt now, because the lions run too fast for me." This simple but wise gesture had a tremendous impact on the son, the hunter and the hunter's family. If the hunter had kept on hunting, he would eventually have come home without food for his family. By handing on the spear, he gives new talent a chance. He passes on his experience and wisdom, whilst at the same time earning the respect of his son and the rest of his relatives. Survival of the entire family (himself included) is more important than his personal status as a hunter.

In the modern business world, it seems that we have forgotten this 'generation pact', because we live with the illusion that we are safe. Even the oldest hunter thinks that he can find enough food to help his company or organisation to survive. We think that we can end our professional career on the highest rung of the ladder without any problem. This seems to be the goal of most of us, but we seldom realise how much hunting talent we are holding back with out selfishness – even though the young are ready to hunt and can actually now hunt better than us.

The truth is that we do <u>not</u> live in a safe environment. New competitors are starting to use sources of energy which we once thought were exclusively at our disposal. They are delivering products and services to customers who we once thought were exclusively ours. This did not happen overnight – or without warning. In a statement from the European Commission as far back as 1992, we can read: "New competitors are entering the market and they are capable of assimilating our technological developments." But the old hunters do not want to see the danger. They only live for reaching – and keeping – the highest position in the hierarchy. They have lost sight of the need for 'collective' survival.

Europe has slowly become a region under pressure. Part of the problem is that we fail to stimulate flexible promotion for people with 'the right skills'. Our natural 'skills life cycle' has ceased to function – the progress of the young is blocked by a rusty phalanx of senior managers and experts. Even the worlds of education, social profit, the unions and politics fall victim to this phenomenon. The spears are passed down to the next generation far too slowly. Those at the top rely on a false sense of security.

What now? A new generation pact is unavoidable: a project to encourage an influx of the right talents, abilities and skills. If this happens, it could also provide solutions to other challenges as well. More women will be promoted, more young talent, more immigrant talent, more physically disabled talent – perhaps even older, as yet unused, talent. Who knows?

Does this mean that we should push aside and dismiss the older generation in its entirety? Absolutely not. In this new generation pact, older people in the 'wrong' role will evolve into a different role. Even the transition from an active career to more free time can happen in a balanced way – or did you think that the hunter who passes down his spear has nothing to do any more?

Can it be done differently? No, it *has* to be done differently –
because the lions are running faster.

MY DEGREE ISN'T WORTH ANYTHING ANY MORE

In many organisations, people with a bachelor or a masters degree
often obstruct organisational developments where actual skills are
more important than university degrees. Most of the time, this
kind of resistance cannot be rationally defended. These are the last
convulsions of a 2D-organisation, desperately trying to stay alive.
Impressive-sounding (but ultimately meaningless) titles are the
ideal defence mechanism in this environment.

The list of possible self-justifications is long and becomes ever-
more personal, more emotional and more irrational:
- It's not my idea.
- I don't like the guy who came up with the idea.
- He did something bad to me once.
- I want to end my career on the highest rung of the ladder.
- I can't afford to be making mistakes.
- I haven't been involved from the start.
- I am the boss...

When faced with comments of this kind, there is little point in
trying to work out the rationality behind this resistance to change.
Look instead for the personal interests of the Red Monkey Hunters: this is where you will find an explanation for their obstruction
of new ideas and their murder of Red Monkeys. This also helps to
explain why conflicts in organisations can be so heated when the
renewal of the organisation is under discussion. And that is why

a professional approach to this conflict is absolutely essential – no matter how difficult it might be!

Tactics of the Red Monkey® Hunter

During my career as the Corporate Learning Officer of a large organisation and later as an advisor on organisational development, I have both observed and felt the effects of active Red Monkey Hunter behaviour. Often they act cunningly, to make sure that the organisation does not change. Six typical tactics are:

TACTIC 1 • KILL THE BREEDER

It's very simple: every time someone kills a Red Monkey, they will also try to eliminate the Red Monkey Breeder who introduced it to the jungle; otherwise there is a possibility that the Breeder will come back tomorrow with a new Red Monkey. Of course, our hunter is very subtle about this.

For example, the Red Monkey Hunter might talk to a young mother just after she has given birth. He condescendingly tells her that the baby can't walk, talk or feed itself. It's not even potty-trained. These kinds of humiliating comments – when expressed publicly – might make the mother think twice before giving birth to another baby!

Red Monkey Hunters treat Red Monkeys and their creators in much the same way. They fail to see their potential; only their threat. They think that if the Breeders are publicly humiliated and attacked often enough, they will eventually stop creating new ideas – and might even become Hunters themselves.

TACTIC 2 • ONLY USE SHORT-SIGHTED INTELLIGENCE

It is a matter of honour for Red Monkey Hunters to kill as many Red Monkeys as possible: among hunters this is seen as a sign of 'intelligence'. Perhaps it is, but it is also a sign of short-sightedness. Saying that a baby is not able to walk – thereby implying that it never will – clearly indicates intelligence which is at best myopic and at worst illogical. The basic observation is correct, but it lacks a vision of the future. People with short- sighted intelligence think and act only for the short term. Real 'system thinkers' on the other hand possess an intelligence which can be projected into the long term.

TACTIC 3 • OPENLY SUPPORT OTHER HUNTERS

This tactic rallies a growing group of followers behind the attempts to kill our Red Monkey. The Red Monkey Hunters openly reward other hunters for every head shot. This 'popular' applause incites other hunters still further: it is a form of symbolic approval that cleverly encourages imitative behaviour. If the tactic works, everything gets rapidly out of hand: the Red Monkey Hunters will unite into a nearly unstoppable force. You have probably noticed this phenomenon in meetings where a new idea is introduced: a short- sighted Red Monkey Hunter will fire the first shot, the group laughs – and suddenly our Red Monkey is under threat from a barrage of shots on all sides.

These three tactics are quite aggressive and visible, but the next three are not. They are dirtier and meaner. Instead of rejecting the new idea from the outset, the Red Monkey Hunters will seemingly accept it – only to undermine it later.

TACTIC 4 • DON'T FEED THE RED MONKEY

One of the most subtle hunting techniques is to accept the birth of a Red Monkey. The hunter might even welcome this birth publicly – but then he refuses to feed the monkey, so that it won't be able to mature. This type of hunter feels an intense satisfaction when the baby dies a couple of months later. It even saves him a bullet. All he had to do was wait. Furthermore, he can point to his own 'good will', while criticising creative people as 'dreamers', who are unable to put their ideas into practice.

TACTIC 5 • IGNORE THE RED MONKEY'S EXISTENCE

This tactic is similar to the previous one: simply ignore the confrontational idea. Don't even mention its birth. If managers do this, they know very well what will happen in the long-term : the Red Monkey Breeder will eventually stop talking about it as well.

TACTIC 6 • OPENLY ENCOURAGE THE BREEDER, BUT...

Sometimes it is enough to openly congratulate and encourage the breeder. There is a common expression about innovation which runs: "If it is a good idea, it will succeed on its own. If it is a bad idea, it will disappear by itself." This is an easy solution for management: Red Monkey Breeders will have to overcome so many obstacles and pitfalls before their idea succeeds that most of them give up.

This situation can be compared to an athlete with explosive sprint potential who has to make all his non-sporting preparations himself: he has to look for sponsors, compose training schedules, monitor his health and general condition, etc. How many modern athletes are able to do this?

In organisations, it is often said that someone quits or performs badly because they lack 'perseverance', whereas it is actually the Red Monkey Hunter who has done everything (or nothing) to prevent the Breeder from getting his idea off the ground. The best athletes do not always have good business instincts and Red Monkey Breeders are not always the best entrepreneurs. In just the same way an athlete might think about the next race before he has barely finished his last one, Breeders think about new ideas when they have only just launched their previous one. There are only a rare few of the species who can succeed in completing the entire process of creative entrepreneurship. It's a pity really: you lose a lot of fantastic sprinters that way!.

Creative entrepreneurship can be prevented by an initial lack of creativity or by a intentional lack of entrepreneurship.

Using these last three tactics during a hunt for Red Monkeys is the easiest way by far: simply refuse the Red Monkey Breeder all help. These tactics also get rid of any uneasy feeling of premeditated murder.

PERVERTED HUNTING BEHAVIOUR:
LOOK FOR A SURROGATE MOTHER

Managers and employees who are active in an organisation where Red Monkey Hunters rule the roost eventually stop proposing new ideas. The fear of failure and non-survival is too great.

The most striking example that I experienced of this as a training manager, was when a top executive asked me to find an external consultant who could put the company on the road to becoming a "service-driven company". In the future, the company didn't just want to sell products, but services as well. This would mean that drastic changes in the organisational chart would be necessary at all levels. After he had explained to me perfectly how a service-driven company should work, I asked him why he didn't propose the idea to his colleagues himself. After all, I thought that this was his task: to develop a vision *and* to convey it. His answer was amazing – and incomprehensible. He feared that his direct colleagues, who had the same 'status', would immediately reject the idea. For this reason, he was searching for a 'surrogate mother' for his idea. If the idea was accepted, he could come forward as the creator; if the idea was rejected, he could hunt with the pack. After all, it wouldn't be "his" child...

Red Monkey® Breeders on the counter

Are Red Monkey Breeders completely powerless? Not really. They have developed several tactics to strengthen themselves in response to the opposition they face. In essence, their behaviour doesn't differ all that much from the Red Monkey Hunters'. It is noticeable that their tactics – like those of their opponents – are often based on keeping a low profile. They hide and wait. Or they flee the forest, taking their Red Monkey with them. It remains to be seen whether these are fruitful techniques. The best case scenario for the company is that if the Red Monkey is unconditionally accepted and cherished. In this way, neither the Monkey nor the Breeder become frustrated.

TACTIC 1 • LAUNCH SUBMARINE PROJECTS

Passionate Red Monkey Breeders realise the danger of immediate death in the jungle but they do not give up. Their urge to innovate is so strong that they continue their work underground. They are actually quite ingenious at avoiding Red Monkey Hunters. The Red Monkey is raised secretly, in the hope that no one will discover it until it is mature. The smartest Red Monkey Breeders manage to do this for years. Unfortunately, they are in grave danger. When this type of 'submarine' project is discovered, harsh accusations will be made: misuse of resources, lack of loyalty to the company, etc... Sadly, management does not realise that they incited this behaviour in the first place.

TACTIC 2 • PUT THE MONKEY ON THE BACK BURNER

Some animals lay their eggs in the mud, to hide them from the prying eyes of predators. These eggs are capable of surviving many years of drought. When a rainy season sweeps over the land, the seemingly extinct species rises again. Some Red Monkey Breeders do something similar – but Red Monkey Breeders don't put their ideas in the mud; they put them in a drawer. They wait for a time when their idea might stand a chance of survival. If this does not happen or if the waiting period is too long, they may move on to tactic 3.

TACTIC 3 • LOOK FOR ANOTHER FOREST

Red Monkey Breeders who have to wait too long will eventually leave the organisation. Most entrepreneurial Red Monkey Breeders become independent and care for their monkey by themselves.

Look around. It happens everywhere. Many motivated young entrepreneurs used to work in big organisations where their Red Monkey Breeder instincts were not nurtured. Their departure represents a huge creative drain for their former employer. That is why it is important for existing organisations to keep these people on board and... spoil them.

DANGER: RED MONKEY BREEDER
BECOMES RED MONKEY HUNTER

Puncturing the 2D-organisation mentality is not easy. It is striking to see how many young businesses founded by dissident Red Monkey Breeders never go onto become 3D-organisations. The cause is fairly obvious: the habit of transferring so-called 'best practices' from old to new organisations is fraught with difficulties. Big companies tend to be 2D-organisations, with a majority of Red Monkey Hunters. They are very stable systems, with processes which affirm the values of the old culture. At the other end of the spectrum, we find young organisations with Red Monkey Breeders. They want to grow but they don't have the necessary experience to evolve from a small to a large 3D-organisation – and so they ask for advice from 'old masters'. And where can these old masters be found? In old 2D-organisations, of course! Consequently, the young Red Monkey Breeders unconsciously copy negative processes which empower the Red Monkey Hunters in their own organisation. Perhaps they even become hunters themselves. Involuntarily, they contribute to the rigidity of their own organisational mentality.

AN ANSWER TO THE 3D CHALLENGE: RED MONKEY® POLITICS

Conclusion: the destructive tendencies of Red Monkey Hunters

Is there anything wrong with stability? No. Stable systems keep each other in balance. The jungle will not react if there are no Red Monkeys to disturb the ecobalance or upset the other monkeys,

However, Red Monkeys *do* exist. They are infiltrating organisations at an ever increasing speed, And because these organisations allow Red Monkeys, they are evolving quickly toward new and better forms of organisation, which are much smarter and react more efficiently to the world's changes. The world's biggest 'patent machines' are no longer the traditional industrial countries, but the newcomers who have turned constant innovation almost into a hobby.

As long as organisations remain unchanged and as long as the market system stays in balance, there will be no competition. In the 21st century, however, this global balance has been disturbed. In the new information and innovation era, organisations are being forced to look for a new balance.

Red Monkey Hunters oppose this mission. But instead of helping their organisation, they are actually condemning it to decline and death. They do not realise that they are digging their own graves. Ultimately, their actions lead to self-destruction, especially in the organisations where they form the majority.

Some basic understanding of Darwinism can help us to clarify this process. Darwin understood that all living organisms develop through an evolutionary process to their present state. New species come into existence by natural selection. If you put this theory into the context of the business world, it is clear that organisations which do not adapt are doomed to disappear.

Luckily, Red Monkey Breeders have developed tactics which can partially protect their ideas, but they are not always sufficient. Top managers also have the responsibility to protect Red Monkey Breeders and their Red Monkeys. To do this, they need to master the ideas and techniques of Red Monkey Politics. The following chapters are dedicated to discussing this crucial issue.

6 Red Monkey® Politics: practice

Introduction

The film *The Last of the Mohicans* contains a scene that perfectly illustrates what could happen if you don't transform your 2D-organisation into a 3D-one on time. A group of English soldiers, led by Lieutenant Ambrose, is crossing the forest. In the middle of the woods the Red Coats are attacked by Huron Indians. Five English soldiers die immediately. Lieutenant Ambrose shouts orders and his soldiers line up to fire in the direction of the first attack. Meanwhile, they are assailed from left and right as well: the Hurons do not fight in a single group but in quick teams of two or three warriors, where one Huron can cover the others. Ambrose keeps giving orders: "Load... shoulder... fire..." But before a single soldier can shoot, four more are dead.

How can a trained army be surprised and slaughtered in this way? The answer is obvious: the British army – in this case, a platoon headed by Lieutenant Ambrose – was not capable of defending itself against an enemy with an innovative strategy. The same thing happened to the American army in Vietnam. Young, modern companies employ similar tactics to attack large, established companies.

Until recently, this inability to deal with new threats from innovative sources was merely a temporary problem. The British finally conquered America and eventually killed off the Hurons – but only after much bloodshed.

Nowadays, things are not so simple. New ideas and new tactics appear faster and find their way more quickly into the mainstream. The war on terrorism is one contemporary example; the constant pressure on record companies to completely restyle the sale of popular music is another. Record companies complain that piracy reduces their profits, but they fight this piracy with completely outdated methods. What they should be doing is changing their products, their commercial model *and* their organisation to counteract or even anticipate piracy.

How do you change these things? How do you make sure that your successful company keeps up with emerging trends, so that you might become the market leader again? As Peter Senge, one of the founders of the 'learning organisation' principle once said: how does an organisation retain "the capability to create its own future". This is only possible by creating organisations where the Red Monkey Breeders have the advantage – and this inevitably means by adopting Red Monkey Politics.

The players enter the arena

An observation: in every organisation there are Red Monkey Hunters (most of the time they are in the majority), but also Red Monkey Breeders. If this is not the case, the organisation is already dead. A 3D-organisation which wants to ensure continuous innovation has to make certain that the breeders get sufficient opportunities and adequate access to information. It needs to restore the natural innovation process. This process is all about power and conflict: the power of the strongest and the skill of the most cunning... In many ways, it is like politics. And just like real politics, this conflict involves more than one party or actor. Faced with this situation, the options are either to attack each other or form a coalition. The way coalitions are formed within an organisation will determine the success or stagnation of the innovation process.

The different actors involved in this drama are the creators, the pioneers, the followers and the settlers.

CREATORS: AUTHENTIC RED MONKEY BREEDERS

Creators are the suppressed minority within the ruling organisational structure. They live at the very edge of the organisation, at the border of the jungle. Now and then they plunge into the stormy waters of information, where all modern organisations are active. Many creators live a second, hidden life. They are the windows of the organisation onto the chaos of the world. Time and again, they discover new insights and new information, which enables them to undermine accepted ways of thinking. They launch challenging new ideas and prototypes.

Red Monkey Breeders are a window onto the chaos of the world. They have their fingers on the pulse of the world.

However, the creators also have a drawback: they rarely finish a job. Their ideas and prototypes often have defects, raise questions or contain errors. In a 2D-organisation this is usually enough to neutralise and eliminate their ideas. In contrast, 3D-organisations try to provide support for creators, by turning to a second group for help. Instead of suddenly releasing their defenceless Red Monkeys into the centre of the jungle, creators in 3D-organisations invite possible friends to pay them a maternity visit. If you have this kind of creator in your organisation, support them. If you don't have them, start looking for them immediately.

PIONEERS: JUST WHAT THE CREATORS NEED

Pioneers are not real Red Monkey Breeders. You could call them Red Monkey Lovers. They are not capable – as their friends, the creators, are – of coming up with new ideas over and over again but they *do* recognize a good idea when they see it. They are also immediately enthusiastic and are eager to visit the maternity ward – and no, they don't gossip the moment they leave the room about what an ugly baby it is. To them, all babies are beautiful.

Pioneers are the incubators for small and defenceless Red Monkeys.

Pioneers are open to confrontational ideas, but they realise that the ideas themselves are just the beginning. They are like the real pioneers of the old Wild West: they explore possibilities and seek to overcome practical barriers. Pioneers are also capable of making contact with creators outside the jungle: use this to your advantage if you don't have any creators in your own organisation. The chance of finding a creator elsewhere will only increase if you broaden your own horizons.

FOLLOWERS:
THE DOUBTING THOMAS'S OF YOUR ORGANISATION

"Except I can see..., I will not believe!" So said Thomas the Apostle in the Bible. Pioneers are imaginative enough to understand how something might work in the future. A semi-completed idea is enough for them; they will develop it further until it works. Followers are incapable of this. They do not tolerate mistakes: the idea must function without any problems from the start. "Under construction" is unacceptable!

> *Followers must see it; pioneers only need to believe in it.*

But the Doubting Thomas's are not Red Monkey Hunters. They are sceptical at first but they are prepared to support a truly worthwhile innovation, once they know what it is for and what advantages it can offer. But there is a danger: followers can be easily influenced. They are blown by the wind. When your organisation is dominated by settlers (our final group), it will be difficult to get the followers to support new plans.

SETTLERS: THE REAL DANGER

Settlers are almost immovable. They think that none of this 'innovation nonsense' is necessary. Everything was going okay, wasn't it? Settlers don't believe in change and are therefore the only real Red Monkey Hunters in your organisation. They shoot at anything that even remotely resembles a Red Monkey.

> *Red Monkey Hunters gather their ammunition from the successes of the past – and shoot the future to pieces.*

The behaviour of settlers, is largely controlled by their emotions and personal feelings,. That is why it is almost impossible to reason with them. Their various arguments were summarised in chapter 5, where the profile of the Red Monkey Hunter was defined in detail. How do you deal with them inside your organisation? There is sometimes a small chance that settlers will reluctantly agree to a change, especially if it is supported by the followers. However, if this does not happen, there is only one solution: curb their power.

A matter of relationships

These four categories are (of course) somewhat arbitrary. A follower is never just a follower and a pioneer is not always a pioneer. A creator might not remain a creator for his entire life. Moreover, the four groups have certain rules and conventions which define and influence their mutual relationships. You might already have noticed the special relationship, for example, between followers and settlers.

If you look more closely at this matter, the fact that no one ever belongs to a single category on a permanent basis should encourage you: it means that increasing the number of Red Monkey Breeders in your organisation is within the realms of possibility. Even settlers are not just settlers for ever. Sometimes you simply need to know what a settler likes in order to involve him in the group. Knowing this will help you to find him a new and challenging role (at least in his eyes). He might not become a creator or even a pioneer, but he could become a follower.

It is for this reason that you must always keep in mind that our destiny as a creator or a settler is not predetermined. Generally, it is the environment which determines how people react towards change and innovation. Creating the right environment is therefore of the utmost importance.

> *People are like chameleons. They become creator, pioneer, follower or settler, depending upon the environment in which they live.*

Furthermore, there are also some individuals who belong to more than one category simultaneously. For example, a creator can also have pioneer blood. It can be difficult to keep these people on board, because often they want to raise their Red Monkey all by themselves. A possible solution to this problem is to create a spin-off for them, where they can have free rein. You must always be careful, however, to ensure that this creator does not transform into a settler, because he likes 'his' baby better than all the other babies in the nursery.

It can get even more complicated. A creator can sometimes be a settler: not for his own idea, but for someone else's idea. In other words, the categories of settler and creator are not fixed and time-bound. Depending on the circumstances, it is possible for someone to belong to any of these four groups.

In short, these categories are a guide: so do not use them as hard and fast indicators. It is important to accept that people are fickle. It is even more important to know what lies behind the position that they are taking. If you can discover this, you can start building a 3D-organisation. And don't forget to look at yourself! As a manager you must also be flexible and react quickly to anything that happens both inside and outside your organisation. This will not be possible if you have fixed ideas: you need to think openly and look for patterns.

Networking, lobbying and forming coalitions

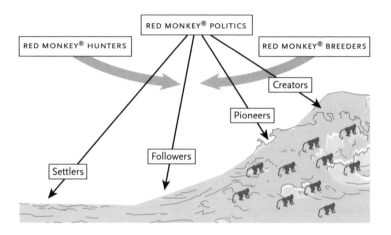

Figure 4 · *Creators and pioneers battle with settlers for the favour of the followers*

In the previous paragraph, we learnt that you should never put individuals in a single category. This is important to know in understanding how innovation processes in your organisation can be stimulated and implemented. A second aspect that you always need to keep in mind are the numerous relationships – the networks – which operate at the battle front between the Red Monkey Breeders and the Red Monkey Hunters.

In figure 4, the four categories are symbolically presented. On the far right, you can see the creators or Red Monkey Breeders. On the left, you can find the settlers or Red Monkey Hunters. The followers and pioneers form the front between them. It almost goes without saying that all these groups lobby, network and even form coalitions with one another.

It is never the case that the creators (Red Monkey Breeders) immediately form coalitions with followers; they need the pioneers for that. Furthermore we have seen that creators can occasionally behave like settlers. Consequently, there can sometimes be danger even from among your own peer group: creators have been known to eliminate each other. Pioneers can help by acting as negotiators and mediators. The interplay of all these possible alliances and relations (sometimes even three-cornered relationships) is called Red Monkey Politics. It is just like real politics: very complex and requiring a lot of effort and perseverance!

To become an innovative 3D-organisation, you need to devise a strategy to facilitate the acceptance of more and more Red Monkeys. Some factors will help with this; some factors will work against it. The 'power of vision' is an example of the former and the 'power to resist' is an example of the latter. But there is a third factor as well: the 'power to change'. Power to change is an ally of power of vision – and it is neutralised by power to resist. The interaction of these three forces decides whether innovative ideas will succeed or not. It is a kind of trench warfare, where the front is shifting continuously.

VISION POWER: CREATORS AND PIONEERS AS WAVE MAKERS

Contrary to what you might think, creators do not have a monopoly on an organisation's power of vision. In fact, this power only

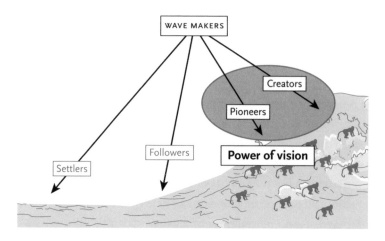

Figure 5 · *The dialogue between creators and pioneers fuels the organisation's power of vision.*

exists when creators and pioneers work closely together and find a constructive synergy.

Creators have a unique connection with the outside world, but remain loyal to the organisation. They frequently present new insights to the pioneers at the 'home base'. This makes creators an indispensable link for vision power. Thanks to their outward-looking mentality on the one hand and their internal collaboration with the pioneers on the other hand, they do indeed secure the future of the organisation; but they cannot do it alone. It is the entrepreneurial pioneers who fuse the new insights with the reality of the organisational structure and consequently help to define the scope and power of the vision.

The synergy between these two groups creates a picture of the future which is continuously adjusted by further new insights.

The creators introduce Red Monkeys at the edge of the jungle. The pioneers raise these new, vulnerable Red Monkeys until they are strong enough to take their place at the heart of the jungle.

Pioneers have the respect of the creators: so much, that pioneers have permission to shoot their Red Monkeys, if necessary.

Pioneers have the necessary judgement to be able to estimate the monkey's likely chances of survival. If a Red Monkey does not satisfy the needs of the organisation, pioneers may be forced to kill it. However, they never do this in the same manner as the settlers. These Red Monkey Hunters kill out of personal interest or for other emotional reasons. The pioneers do it based on sound arguments. Their most important task is to ensure that the creator understands and is convinced by these arguments. If they do not succeed, the creator may go elsewhere. This means one less Red Monkey Breeder in the organisation and a further disruption of the innovative balance.

In other words, the engine of innovation is powered on one side by the creators' new insights, derived from perceived trends, and on the other side by the pioneers' pragmatic attitude. The better an organisation is able to recognise new trends and new insights, the stronger its vision will be. And the strong vision usually means a better strategy for driving innovation. The resulting passion for new ideas will eventually infect the entire organisation.

Creators and pioneers are close allies. Together they can constantly make new waves of innovation. Pioneers act as a sounding board for the creators. They stimulate them to conceive new Red Monkeys over and over again. Pioneers are very tolerant of errors in the initial ideas. They translate these errors into new challenges for the creators, so that they can look for further improvements. On the other hand, pioneers are useless on their own: they need to have at least one creator providing them with inspiration. If a pioneer faces a practical challenge, he can always ask the creator for help. This means that the pioneers are demanding – but always motivating – managers. They are the champions of the creators and the entrepreneurs who turn their creative ideas into reality.

CHANGING POWER:

PIONEERS AND FOLLOWERS AS WAVE SURFERS

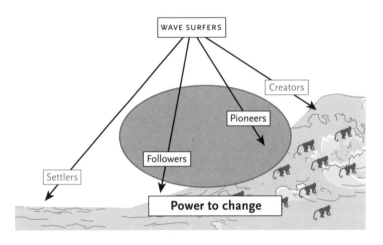

Figure 6 · *The power of the pioneers to convince the followers will determine the 'power to change' of an organisation*

If creators and pioneers make waves, there are always people who are prepared to surf on them. These are the followers. It is clear that the work of the creators and the pioneers will not be much use without the followers. This is why followers are the necessary third group in the triangular relationship which makes innovation in your organisation possible.

Followers will never surf on their own. They wait to see what happens. Pioneers have the talent to involve the followers in change. They can translate the necessary innovation into the life and everyday working world of people who like to 'work' and who are open to a new approach. However, the change must be a proven success, since followers only like to be involved in change when they understand why it is necessary. In this respect, followers are not always easy to deal with. They often realise that the organisation needs to adapt to the quickly changing world, because it will not survive otherwise. Yet they are sceptical and they do not like improvisation or games – and games are what Red Monkeys love! An idea has to grow – and to grow it, you need to play with it. This is what creators and pioneers do. How else can they discover the full possibilities of the idea? Followers don't like this. For them, a new Red Monkey idea needs to be able to 'deliver' immediately.

To indicate the general direction, you need creators and pioneers.
To truly change the organisation, you need followers.

In the triangular relationship between creators, pioneers and followers, the pioneers act as the buffer. They provide the incubator which keeps the Red Monkeys alive. Direct contact between the creator and the followers can often be fatal for the infant Red Monkey. Generally, there are more fights than communication between these two groups. The creator blames the followers for being short-sighted and not open to creativity. The followers are annoyed because the creator does not have any practical insights into their daily problems. They think that he lives in a fantasy world: as a result, his beautiful new ideas might never come to fruition.

The creators should be viewed as discoverers of a new world. They explore uncharted territories and return with magnificent stories about the opportunities of the fabulous new lands. Pioneers immediately see the advantages and set off to exploit these new lands. When they return with ships loaded with gold and grain, they are able to encourage the followers to cross the ocean. For an organisation with a sound process of innovation, this part of the cycle is easily recognisable. This is when change really begins to happen. In short, the balance in the relationship between creator – pioneer – follower (especially if the pioneers have a lot of influence), is the source of the changing power in your organisation.

RESISTANCE POWER: SETTLERS AS WAVE BREAKERS

But there is always danger! Just like the triangular relationship between creators, pioneers and followers, there is also an equally subtle association between pioneers, followers and settlers. In the former, the pioneers are the decisive factor. Their power to eliminate weak Red Monkeys without alienating the creator and to convince followers to accept the surviving monkeys is the key to innovative success.

In this second triangular relationship – between pioneers, followers and settlers – something else is taking place. Followers (naturally enough) follow – and they are willing to follow anyone. At first, they will often pick the easy option and side with the settlers.

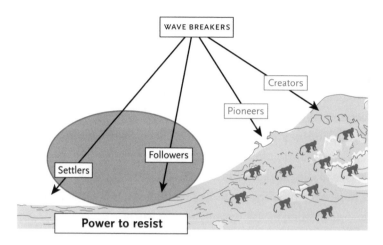

Figure 7 · *When settlers paralyse and contaminate followers, their joint power to resist will prevail*

This is because the settlers are excellent at networking and convincing others. Instead of jumping on the barricades to resist the innovation themselves, the settlers allow the followers to do it for them. The word "we" is a powerful weapon. Self-interest is their motive. Re-read chapter 5 about Red Monkey Hunters, if you want to understand how the settlers operate.

Networks are ever present. The strongest network wins.

The easiest followers to influence are those who are not sure whether to go along with innovation or to wait. We have already talked about a 'front line' and it is clear that this is where the battle will be the bloodiest. If the influence of settlers is strong, then the waves of innovation will be broken. In today's rapidly changing environment, this will mean that the organisation's survival is in peril. If the pioneers are able to win, the chances of survival are significantly increased.

For this reason, it is very important for an organisation to keep the group of followers as large as possible. This requires great effort because (as has already been explained) followers can change sides in the blink of an eye. One moment they may be leaning towards the camp of the pioneers, whereas the next moment they may decide to join the settlers instead. Consequently, the pioneers have a huge responsibility: the task of neutralising resistance power in an organisation by influencing the followers.

But followers can also play a key role as a buffer between the pioneers and the settlers. Usually, there is no communication between these latter two groups. Pioneers consider the settlers to be a lost cause. Only the followers can change this. The more followers an organization has, the more difficult it will be for the settlers to hold their ground. If they want to stay on board, they will need to adapt and sail with the new wind.

MIDDLE MANAGEMENT AS SETTLER

In my experience, it is not always the fault of the ordinary employees that innovation is so difficult to implement. All too often, the root cause of the problem can be found in middle management, which plays a very dubious part in the entire process of change and innovation. Necessary modernisations often have an immediate impact on middle management – whether on their role as managers (their 'organisational character') or on their status as experts (their 'technical expertise').

In both cases the possible consequences are sufficient to convert these managers into zealous settlers. In their existing functions, they can influence a lot of employees. The way in which they do this is not always clear. Most of the time they are very articulate but, being settlers, they are not actively involved in innovation. Even so, their attitude quickly contaminates their employees. Unfortunately, middle managers often think first and foremost of themselves – only then do they think of the organisation.

Let this be a warning to every organisation that wants to create a strongly embedded innovation dynamic. An important aspect will be the careful selection of middle management, in order to ensure that this key level fully supports innovation. The middle manager must stimulate his team's urge to innovate, even if this endangers his own position. Middle managers need to promote the interests of the organisation, not their own careers. They need to develop a balanced approach to change which can aid the creators and the pioneers, but without neglecting operational responsibilities.

Conclusion: moving the front...

Just like in politics, business organisations have different parties with opposing interests. In innovation processes, you will find the Red Monkey Breeders on one side and the Red Monkey Hunters on the other.

Red Monkey Breeders can usually be found in the creator and pioneer groups within the organisation. Red Monkey Hunters generally form the settler group. The follower group stands between these two power blocks and they will join either the breeders or the hunters.

In this sense, the innovation process in your organisation is neither a procedure nor an implemented (management) system. You cannot look at the process without looking at the relationships between the different groups in your organisation: creators, pioneers, followers and settlers.

Pioneers and creators together are the vehicles for the power of vision, which is a necessary condition for innovation. They see a new future and the pioneers in particular can be very convincing at telling the 'story', showing the possibilities and providing successful examples.

Creators and pioneers use their power of vision to convince the followers to join them. This is the changing power, originating from the cooperation between these three groups. It is this power which can turn your organisation into a truly creative enterprise.

On the other side of the fence are the settlers – dogged networking veterans – who obstruct the innovation process with their paralysing resistance power. They, too, need the support of the followers to accomplish their mission. The front line of innovation is located at the point where proponents and opponents of change meet. The side which is best at networking and at convincing the most followers is the side which will win. If the settlers are the strongest group, the organisation will capsize and sink. If the creators – with the invaluable help of the pioneers – can triumph, the organisation will be able to find a new course for the future.

This paints a painfully clear picture of the drama of a 2D-organisation: in such organisations, change is guided by the desire to improve existing processes. This does not involve a great deal of innovation. In the 3D-era, where change and innovation happen at a much faster pace, the 2D-organisation will not suffice. The number of Red Monkey Breeders – people with revolutionary and innovative insights – has to be increased dramatically. The fight to win the followers will be bloody and brutal – but the front must shift to the advantage of the Red Monkey Breeders.

In chapter 7 I will explain how you can keep Red Monkeys alive in your organisation. It is time to step into the world of Red Monkey Innovation Management.

7 Red Monkey® Innovation Management: the necessary condition

Introduction

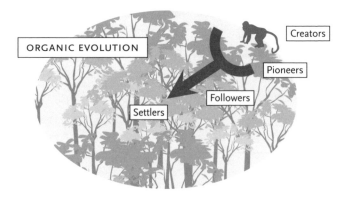

Figure 8 · *Change processes start with creators and pioneers at the 'edge' of the organisation*

Change processes in an organisation should not be introduced top-down. Changes have to be carefully channelled if you want them to be successful. Perhaps the analogy of a channel is not a good one: it is actually more like a river bed, since changes never follow the exact same route. You have read in chapter 6 that the actors – creators, pioneers, followers and settlers – do not always fulfil the same role: for one change, person X is a creator but for another change he might be a follower.

Red Monkeys will continue to be born and change will find its way. To see what is really going on, it is necessary to tip over every domino on the path of the change process. Don't try to knock them all down at once, because this will only create chaos, confusion and waste.

The manner in which you carefully tip over each domino, one at a time – each of which introduces new processes of permanent change and innovation into your organisation – is called Red Monkey Innovation Management.

The dominos fall

Red Monkey Innovation Management is an organic process. No one can impose innovation on someone else; it is the result of a silent (r)evolution at the edge of the jungle. Creators come up with an innovative new idea, based on intense contacts with and acute observations of the outside world. The moment the spark of an idea ignites in their brain, they start looking for one or more pioneers who are willing to incubate the idea.

The pioneers have to nurture the idea until it is a working prototype, a 'best practice'. When the prototype has proven its value and shown that it can function with virtually no errors, the followers become the target. The pioneers use the prototype to convince the followers to join the cause of change.

The advantages of this type of Red Monkey Innovation Management should be immediately apparent. Thanks to the organic – some might even say slow – implementation of the new idea, the basic concept has a better chance to anchor itself in the minds of the employees. Instead of dropping the challenging idea into the middle of the jungle, which would increase the chances of it being eliminated straight away, it is released at the edge of your organisation. Equally important, you must choose to release it near to those groups of people who you know will be willing to accept a properly functioning new idea.

When you go about things in this deliberate manner, you must do everything in your power to make sure that the pathway to successful innovation is smooth and free of obstacles. In particular, you should put all available budgetary resources into developing the idea, rather than trying to protect it. You must never be in a hurry. Haste means that the Red Monkey will be shown to the followers before the defence mechanisms of the settlers have been neutralised.

> *Change projects fail because of the wrong people in the wrong place at the wrong time – and not because the idea was bad.*

If you develop the idea calmly and carefully, the result will be more visible to the organisation. The moment the followers understand that they are in a win-win situation, their support for the idea will take off. One by one they will embrace the idea and use it. When these dominos start to fall, it will be almost impossible for the settlers to convince the followers to change their minds back again, because they will *know* that the idea works and that it has advantages. Whether they like it or not, the settlers will have to learn to live with the new-born Red Monkey. In other words, Red Monkey Innovation Management is the only process which can lead to successful and permanent innovation projects (read: confrontational changing routes).

- Budgets are primarily invested in the development of the idea and not in its protection from the settlers.
- The right people with the right attitude appear at the right moment and get 'involved' with the project. Red Monkeys are not always given to the employee with the most time on his hands, because this might be the person who believes least in this specific challenging idea. There is also an additional advantage: the diversity of people who take care of Red Monkey ideas is enormous. This means that everyone can choose according to his or her own personal interests.
- The chances of improving the idea and of creating a working prototype are higher in an organic process. Mistakes are found earlier and repairing them is less costly than if the idea were to be immediately introduced throughout the entire organisation. You never get a second chance for a first impression: if you start off on the wrong foot, there is often no turning back.
- The number of people who truly believe in the idea will steadily increase: there will be a snowball effect, with each person convincing the next one in the chain. Eventually no one will resist, not even the hardcore settlers: all their support will have been undermined.
- Several different Red Monkeys can develop at the same time but in different experimental environments. In 2D-organisations people think and act top-down. Consequently, these

organisations can only have relatively few new processes under consideration at any one time. The majority of these will fail and the costs are huge. At the edge of the jungle – in the 3D-organisation – you can release as many Red Monkeys as you want. There will always be someone who will take care of them. The chances to achieve – and keep achieving – successful innovation increase dramatically.

- Eliminating non-viable Red Monkeys does not have a catastrophic impact: mistakes are detected at an early stage and consequently they do not have a major effect on the organisation, neither financially nor psychologically (because of yet another failed reorganisation).
- Innovation becomes a continuous process, carried out by the right actors. Every process becomes an example for a new process.
- The implementation of an idea seems to be slower but it is more enduring – and therefore quicker in the long run. From a 2D-perspective, 3D-innovation seems slow because the idea is not immediately implemented throughout the entire organisation. However, it is more beneficial – both in terms of time and money – because mistakes do not have dramatic consequences for the whole company.

Conclusion: switch to Red Monkey® Innovation Management

Doesn't it take longer for a Red Monkey project to reach maturity? Can an organisation afford to wait that long before the entire implementation process is completed and the last settler is convinced? This is a valid point, of course. But look at it this way:

if you use Red Monkey Innovation Management, you avoid the mistake of carrying out a change process too quickly (because it was launched top-down) and you are able to innovate successfully with steady organic growth. Which is the better <u>end</u> result? Which route will allow you to reach your end goal the quickest?

Besides, there is another important reason to embrace Red Monkey Innovation Management: the need to transform from the 2D to the 3D-era. As I said at the beginning of this book, change and innovation will be completely different in the next decade. Your organisation will have to transform faster and faster. New business ideas will be introduced into the world and your organisation will have to use them – and get used to them. That's why you will always need more Red Monkeys. The number of Red Monkey Breeders in your organisation must increase drastically – this is the only way to increase the number of ideas – Red Monkeys – which you need to survive.

Innovative ideas with a direct impact on the organisational structure will present themselves at a faster pace. If you throw these Red Monkeys to the lions without carefully preparing yourself through Red Monkey Innovation Management, the consequences could be disastrous. Not only will the Red Monkeys be instantly devoured, but the lions will also become sick from gorging themselves on all that fresh meat!

In the 3D-era, with its barrage of innovation and constant change, an organisation will only remain successful if it evolves into a 3D-organisation. You will need a highly manoeuvrable and battle-ready ship, so that you can adjust your course again and again.

Only a 3D-organisation which uses Red Monkey Innovation Management will be able to do this. Consequently, it is of the utmost importance to switch to Red Monkey Innovation Management as quickly as possible.

PART III

....

RED MONKEY® INNOVATION MANAGEMENT
IN THE 3D-ORGANISATION

8 COMA or COmpany MAlfunction

Introduction

Most wars are lost by armies that are too sure of victory, armies that have never lost a battle and have had one success after another. Totally unexpectedly, they are confronted by a new enemy; an enemy they have never met before; an enemy that uses a completely different strategy. Before they know it, this once victorious army has been decimated. It is their first defeat – but in war (as every general knows) you can only lose once.

This chapter is entitled "COMA". This word is generally used to describe a comatose state that is caused by lack of oxygen to the brain. This is something which can also happen to any inattentive organisation. Organisations lapse into a coma through a lack of information. This lack manifests itself when 2D-managers face a new enemy they have never met before: the 3D-era.

COMA in five steps

A lot of successful organisations from the 2D-era have unconsciously developed a particular management style. The 2D-manager is a manager who always starts from the basic idea that his employees need specific tasks to become and remain active. He is convinced that the organisation will grind to a halt if there is a lack of assignments. A logical consequence of this reasoning is the belief that he (the manager) must always be the smartest person on the team, because otherwise it is impossible for him to give correct and clear instructions. Furthermore, he is convinced that he needs to keep a close check on all the instructions he has given. In the 2D-organisation, the 2D-HR department used this management model to develop a battery of different processes to support employees, managers and senior executives.

BIRTH OF THE 2D-PERSONNEL DEPARTMENT

In 1920, Tead and Metcalf used the following argument to justify the birth of personnel departments within companies: "The fundamental reason for the development of a separate administrative division (personnel department) is a growing recognition that people are endowed with characteristics different from those of machines or raw materials. And if people are to be directed in ways which give the best results, that direction must be specialised, just as the direction in the other major fields of management has been specialized."

This simple argument is still valid in the 2D-organisations of today. The personnel department needs to make sure that employees are used in the best possible way. The only innovation between 1920 and now has been the evolution towards 'people management'. If you treat people humanely, you will get a better result than if you treat them high-handedly. This change in management thinking is what caused the transformation of the 'personnel' department into the 'human resources' department.

In the 2D-era, the task-based mindset was enough for 2D-managers to get things done. But the question arises whether this mindset is still enough, if we are to make the crossing from the 2D-era to the 3D-era. Will the 2D-manager still be capable of getting things done in 3D? We can analyse this question by taking a look at the following five steps.

STEP 1 • THE HEYDAY OF 2D-MANAGEMENT

In the 2D-era, the quantity of information was such that technical experts were able to evolve into 2D-managers without difficulty. These people were usually very talented in their chosen field of expertise and therefore stayed technically more up-to-date than the people they had to manage. They guaranteed a stable 2D-balance in the organisation. The skills of 2D-employees, 2D-managers and 2D-executives completely balanced one another and were supported by 2D-HR processes. Elements which threatened to disrupt the balance were rejected.

STEP 2 • I WORK AT HOME AS WELL,
DAY AND NIGHT IF NECESSARY

As the world evolves towards the 3D-era and as the amount of information which needs to be processed increases substantially, the 2D-manager is no longer capable of learning everything he needs to know during his normal working hours. As a result, he invests some extra 'home' time, just to keep up. He is obliged to make this additional investment because in his 2D-management paradigm he must remain the 'smartest' expert. He believes that his outstanding expertise is what separates him from the others and forms the basis of his authority. In short, it is the reason why he is respected.

But the 2D-manager's work is not over once he has assigned operational tasks to his team. It is expected that he will 'do his bit' to keep the top-down innovation process alive. He might still have the most technical talent, but he nonetheless needs to find the extra time to maintain his technical superiority. He has several options: he can work longer and study more at home (to make sure that his stream of operational tasks is not interrupted); or he can spend less time following up on these tasks; or he can scale down the innovation process; or perhaps he prefers a combination of all three options.

The increasing possibilities to work with a laptop and a smart phone from locations other than the office or factory are promoting work outside office hours even more. This is no longer the exception, it has become the norm.

STEP 3 · THE EMPLOYEES GET RESTLESS

It is clear that the stable 2D-balance will be disturbed by all this frenetic activity. The increase in the amount of information which needs to be processed greatly increases the pressure on the 2D-manager. He is assailed from two sides: on the one side by the incoming stream of new information which he has to study and on the other side by his employees, who become restless as a result of the lack of tasks and guidance. Paradoxically, just at the moment when the organisation needs to react faster and faster, more and more 2D-employees end up doing nothing. They stop getting assignments. Not only do the waiting periods for assignments, progress monitoring and evaluation increase but there are also other side-effects:

- An employee once told me openly that he didn't have any work left to do. Nevertheless, his 2D-manager still claimed that he had a full workload according to his spreadsheet – and that what the spreadsheet said had to be true!.
- 2D-managers under pressure are more likely to give the wrong tasks to the wrong people. This means that they have to retrace their steps at a later stage, frustrating the employees involved. Some become fickle and some – those with short fuses – even become aggressive.
- 2D-employees complain about the performance of their 2D-manager. They say that he has 'lost the plot' completely and just makes changes for the sake of change.

At this stage, it becomes necessary to increase the number of 2D-HR processes as well. The need for formal evaluation and performance interviews will grow. It is yet another way (however unintentional) of putting even more pressure on the management skills of the 2D-manager.

STEP 4 • TRAINING AND PERFORMANCE INTERVIEWS –
THE LAST STRAW

The 2D-top executives now use 2D-HR processes to get the organisation back into line. At this moment, the likelihood that the 2D-manager will have a breakdown is greater than ever. On the one hand, the pressure for him to keep up technically is still growing, while on the other hand the pressure to keep on top of his 2D-management tasks is also growing. This is the beginning of the end for the 2D-manager: the need to carry out performance interviews can often be seen as the last straw. There are examples of 2D-managers who need so much time to prepare for these interviews that they start to hate them – and can no longer see their value. Eventually, the interviews become nothing more than a formality which is simply about awarding points, so that the annual pay rises can be calculated. This allows the 2D-HR department to get its numbers for the completion of the salary calculation spreadsheets – so they will be happy. Provided there are talks about possible training and education courses, the union is happy as well – another one percent of the resources will be spent on (usually useless) training days. Meanwhile the pressure on the manager continues to increase.

The most talented 2D-managers will still be able to filter, process, learn and distribute information. They even will be able to assign tasks and innovate. But the number of these 'successful' 2D-managers will steadily decline. Rarely do 2D-managers in these circumstances notice that more and more of their employees are mentally shutting down, starting to complain and have less and less work to do.

Both 2D-management and 2D-HR services will try to stem the tide – but simply by trying to do the same things as before, only better and faster. This is doomed to fail. Eventually, the 2D-HR processes will collapse. Consider the assignments which the employees are assigned every year: more than half of them never start because of a changing environment. Or think about the rigid competence management systems: these will fail to keep up with the rapid changes in the organisation. The situation is quickly becoming hopeless.

In the 3D-era, 2D-managers either lose sight of reality or refuse to accept it. This 'disease' is then passed on to the 2D-senior executives, to whom the 2D-managers keep reporting that everything is going fine: they have to – otherwise they will get into trouble with their 2D-bosses! I have frequently seen situations where 2D-managers have manipulated their numbers in order to stay in favour with their top manager.

Not only does the stream of tasks stop; but the stream of modernisation dries up as well. The 2D-manager cannot keep up with the developments in his field, or scan emerging information for creative ideas. His role as a creator ceases. The time and insight needed to breed Red Monkeys is long gone.

The biggest drama for organisations is the drying up of the stream of information, whilst they are simultaneously experiencing an information tidal wave.

Innovation power in the 2D-era was already small, because the innovation process started at the top of the organisation. Innovation power is now reduced to zero, because of the meltdown of the 2D-manager. An accelerating ageing process – a direct consequence of the stagnation of the top-down innovation processes – will ultimately result in the end of the organisation. It will lapse into a COMA due to a lack of information. This is the end for the 2D-manager: he is as good as brain dead. The world has changed so quickly from the 2D to the 3D-era that most 2D-managers don't even know why they are no longer doing a good job. For them, it is already too late, but for the organisation there is no time to lose. A new generation of managers is needed!

THE MORAL OF THE STORY

Would Lieutenant Ambrose's Red Coats have been able to fend off the Huron attack if they had worked harder and faster? The answer is a negative; they had been trained to perfection for the execution of specific tasks, but fighting Indians was outside their experience. Ambrose, being a 2D-manager, was simply incapable of processing all the information that he was receiving and he was equally incapable of quickly transforming this information into timely orders for his subordinates. The situation was constantly changing. His orders always came too late. As a manager, he was confronted with a new tactic, from a new era.

Just as Lieutenant Ambrose was incapable of seeing and tracking the movements of the Indians, so the 2D-manager in the 3D-era is incapable of following the trends in his area of expertise. Stress and chaos are the result. His brain goes into meltdown and his head explodes. The 2D-manager's failure in the 3D-world is characterised by indecisiveness and wrong decisions. 2D-employees expect to be directed and controlled. They have no more work and the organisation ends up fighting a losing battle, because the employees no longer have direction. Saddest of all, nobody – at any level in the organisation – can understand what is happening.

Natural evolution

My experience as a training manager and Corporate Learning Officer has taught me one very important lesson: the 2D-manager, no matter how successful he was in the 2D-era, does not stand a chance in the 3D-era. His competences and skills are not suitable for a 3D-role. His environment has changed so radically that other competences and skills are now needed to manage organisations. In short, he is suffering from a clear case of 'Management Malpractice'".

Management malpractice indicates that the competences of a manager are not adapted to the era in which he has to manage. In the 3D-era, the 2D-manager with his 2D-competences has lost control and no longer knows how to manage his team.

MANAGEMENT DRAMA

For 2D-managers in 2D-organisations in the 3D-era, the amount of pressure and stress must be enormous. Once they were the most loyal and most driven managers, always giving of their best. Now they are desperately running around, like a chicken with its head cut off. However, they are not really to blame for the failure of their management practice. The problem lies in the fact that the 2D-organisation has ended up in a 3D-environment – that is the real drama. The celebrated and acclaimed 2D-managers of the past are now, suddenly and unexpectedly, the worst performers. They are trapped in a role in which they cannot hope to succeed, simply because they lack the necessary managerial talents for the 21st century. Ultimately, the manner in which they deal with their own failure and the transition to the 3D-era will decide whether the organisation still has a chance.

Natural evolution into a 3D-organisation

Just as with all other processes of evolution, management is also subject to the principles of natural selection and development. Darwinism is also applicable to companies. The evolution of living organisms can be compared to the evolution of organisations. For the business world, this theory would read as follows: all living companies have gradually evolved into their present state and different species have come into existence through a process of natural selection, driven by market forces.

Put another way: 2D-management is replaced by 3D-management, which drives the development of 3D-organisations. The transition is an organic process, in which two generations of managers stand diametrically opposed to one another. Only when the new generation is given the opportunity to lead the way will the 2D-organisation be able to take a step forward towards the 3D-environment, as part of its natural development process.

The transition from the 2D-era to the 3D-era causes stress and chaos, with three very clear management 'symptoms':

FORM 1 • THROWING UP

This is what happens to the 2D-managers who do not know when to quit. Despite all the signs and omens, these seasick managers continue to give orders and introduce changes. Rare moments of clarity alternate with long periods of dizziness and nausea. Illness can manifest itself in many different forms: from being physically sick to just being grumpy and from mental absence to actual sick leave. These managers will not give up until their heart stops beating.

FORM 2 • LYING DOWN

One cure for seasickness is lying down. Some 2D-managers will become expert at avoiding their management responsibilities. Their influence is only a shadow of what it once was in their heyday. They will survive in the 3D-era as managers, but without any impact: their team members will have to take care of their jobs themselves. They give evasive answers and avoid sensitive issues. Most of the time they are sociable people, who can talk themselves out of any predicament.

Cunning 2D-managers claim that their non-involvement is to allow "the evolution of autonomous teams". Autonomous teams might work in the 2D-era, but not in 3D. The growing number of conflicts within 3D-organisations demands a compelling organisational vision, in order to facilitate the constructive resolution of conflicts. This in turn requires 3D-management and the continuous involvement of the 3D-manager.

FORM 3 • STANDING UP – WITH A NEW VISION!

The other way to overcome seasickness is to bravely stand up on deck and focus on a fictitious point on the horizon. In management terms this is called developing a vision. The development of a vision is the key which can transform 2D-management into 3D-management. It is a magic key which can open the door for new competences to develop. Sadly, most 2D-managers are not equipped with the necessary basic skills to make this happen. Once more Darwin offers us a solution: in a changing environment, only those who change quickly will survive. From the old generation of managers, a new generation will arise; a generation that will discover the importance of vision. These managers will overcome chronic seasickness and give shape to the new 3D-future.

> *In the evolution from 2D-organisations to 3D-organisations, it is not the 2D-managers who will be the guides, but rather the newly emerging 3D-managers – however few they may be.*

Conclusion: birth of the 3D-manager

A species will only survive in a swiftly changing environment if enough of its members can adapt to that new environment. You could say that today's 'abnormalities' are the key to the future.

Deploy this metaphor in your organisation and you will understand that failure to adapt quickly enough to the 3D-era will ensure the organisation's disappearance from the face of this planet. An organisation can only survive when a new generation of managers takes the helm. To do this, the future 3D-managers need to develop completely different competences in comparison with their predecessors. Technical expertise will become less important. Managers will have to find another way to get things done. One of the possible solutions is to develop a long-term vision instead of a short-term view.

The competence to develop a vision will be a key element in the transformation process into 3D-organisations. However, it is not the only competence that will be needed. In chapter 9, I will compare the 2D-manager and his competences with the new 3D-manager.

9 The new 3D-management

Introduction

If you look up the verb 'to manage' in a dictionary, you will find that some of the definitions are surprisingly simple. Essentially, it means 'to get something done' or (a touch more colloquially) 'to pull something off', in the sense of to achieve something. In other words: a good manager 'pulls it off' and makes something happen with a group of colleagues. By extension, this also means that a bad manager fails to get things done.

This simple definition comforts me in my quest to find an answer to the question of why so many attempts at change end so disastrously. 'Managing' is not as obscure as you might think. Managing is simply the art of getting something done. If you can't do that, you fail as a manager. End of story.

In the next few chapters you will see why 2D-managers will not be able to get their job done in the 3D-era. You will understand how and why they will lose their management competences – or even more importantly, why 2D-management competences which were so successful in a 2D-organisation in the 2D-era will be completely useless in the 3D-era. You will discover that successful management in a 3D-organisation needs completely different skills and processes. Let me warn you immediately that this has far-reaching consequences for many current 2D-managers. Many will have to leave the stage as manager! And fast!

This does not only apply to middle managers (as we discussed earlier). Top executives can also be totally dislocated by this phenomenon, if they continue to operate with 2D-competences.

Getting it done... on three levels

It is incorrect to assume that only managers manage. You need to be very clear about this, because in the 3D-organisation *every* employee must skilfully 'pull it off' – and at every level. Self-management will become increasingly important in the future and executives and entrepreneurs who fail to realise this will never be able to create a 3D-organisation.

To innovate successfully and to clearly interpret what will follow, you need to understand the different levels of management within an organisational structure.

TOP MANAGERS (executives) are responsible for the organisation as a whole. In practical terms, this means that they steer the processes which mould a coherent organisation and ensure that all the different teams work together as a single identity. In other words: top managers are people who 'get it done' by making all the teams in an organisation work together as a whole. To do this, they introduce and maintain processes. They give the organisation a future and they stand at the top of the hierarchy, because their impact on the organisation is the biggest. Top managers manage the organisation, other managers, the employees – and themselves. Or, at least, that should be the case...

THE MANAGER 'gets it done' by working together with a team of employees and by accomplishing the team's mission within the organisation in the best possible manner. These men and women are the bridge between top management and employees. In the 3D-organisation, they succeed in making very flexible teams work together with other teams in a series of ever-changing processes. In the context of this book, you need to use the widest possible definition of the term 'manager'. For example, project leaders are also managers.

EMPLOYEES are managers as well – in their own way. This is even more the case in 3D-organisations. Employees are people who excel in their particular speciality. They work 'on the floor'. They are experts. Without them, there is no organisation, no products, no services, no income and no future. In creative organisational cultures they take the responsibility of managing themselves: self-management. Someone with a healthy dose of self-management 'gets it done' by realising their personal and organisational goals.

The 3D-manager versus his old 2D-colleague

The difference in the management competences needed for a 2D-and a 3D-manager is well illustrated in the following example:

Imagine you are planning to buy a new cupboard for your living room. A lot of people have problems imagining how the cupboard would look, so they pile up boxes to get at least an abstract visual impression of the end result. A much smaller group of people is able to simply imagine the three-dimensional visual effect with no effort.

Another example: Imagine you want to paint your living room in a new colour. Many people are totally incapable of picturing the effect of a new colour in their mind, They need a colour sample at the very least. For others, even that is not enough. They paint some strips of their chosen colour on the wall. And even then, they will often sigh and moan that 'the colour is not what they thought it would be'. Only a very small number of people are capable of immediately imagining the entire room in the chosen colour, with almost no information.

In both examples, it is only the last, relatively small group of people who have 3D-potential. But for managers in the 3D-era it is not a question of shapes or colours: it is about the impact of your actions over time. What is the effect of what you are doing now on the future of the organisation and its employees? You can't resort to tricks like piling up boxes or using a colour chart – these are the strategies of the past.

Intuition and vision are the only tools at your disposal. In the old 2D-era there was still a competitive advantage for organisations which improved themselves more quickly than their rivals. Moreover, it was not necessary to think in the long-term in order to improve constantly. The facts and figures said everything and gave guidance as to where (or whether) the organisation should invest. The correct decisions were based on trustworthy information contained in the all-sacred spreadsheets.

In the 3D-era this is no longer the case. From now on, you and your managers need to make decisions based on a long-term vision, using plenty of assumptions and a whole lot of intuition! Managers in the 3D-era need enormous imagination. Simulations no longer work. It's all about being able to make the correct decisions intuitively with not sufficient information. This is creative entrepreneurship.

Let's study this more closely, by comparing the competences which were expected from the 2D-manager in the past and the competences which the 3D-manager needs today.

The 2D-manager's competences

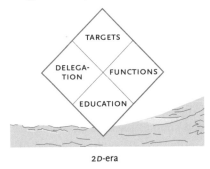

2D-era

Figure 9 · *Expected competences of the 2D-manager*

In the 2D-era, the 2D-manager not only needed the right technical competences, but also four key management competences (figure 9). These were the competence to (1) formulate targets; (2) develop function descriptions; (3) organise training and education; (4) delegate responsibilities.

Before we examine these required managerial competences, it may be useful to say a few words about technical competences, since this is a major problem for a lot of 2D-managers today. In the past, such men and women became managers because of their technical baggage. It was believed that they could learn real management skills as they gained experience. Or not... Throughout their entire career, their superior technical knowledge lifted them above the rest of the team and was the source of their authority. Today, however, many young employees are technically superior to their managers. You can compare this to the situation in education, where students are now better informed about PC and Internet-related issues than their teachers.

Yet even today, managers are still being chosen on the basis of their technical knowledge, their age and their qualifications. The ruinous effect that these 2D-managers can have on their employees is beyond imagination. Nevertheless, the 2D-manager often stays in charge. When I became a training manager in the last decade of the previous century, organisations spent vast amounts of money on training and courses for their 2D-managers. All efforts to sharpen their so-called 'people skills' (their skills in coaching people) had barely any effect and even today most 2D-managers focus primarily on staying ahead of the game, of being the expert they have always been. Their biggest concern is knowing more than their staff: this is their main concern when they talk about 'personal development'. The development of true people skills comes, at best, in second place. As a result, the majority of 2D-managers are sadly lacking these key skills. Perhaps they don't have the talent for it, but you shouldn't blame them. When I became a Corporate Learning Officer, it dawned on me that not only 'training' but *all* HR processes were developed to support the 2D-manager as an expert first and a people manager second. In other words, both the HR processes and the employees adapted themselves to the manager's behaviour. Together they created 2D-organisation cultures.

This meant that 2D-employees in the 2D-era simply needed to develop competences that were complementary to the competences of the 2D-manager. In short, they just had to be smart assistants.

> 2D-*managers do not see their employees as partners: they see them as assistants.*

They were like soldiers in the army: perfectly trained to carry out their commanding officer's orders. Higher up, the general carefully observed the troops and their movements – and the movements of their enemy, as well. He had a good vantage point and if he was capable of making good decisions quickly, he became a successful general (like Nelson or Napoleon). This was how things worked in the 2D-era. The team's speed of reaction was adequate, but only as long as the manager could follow the 'war game'. Victories were only attributed to the highest officer: after all, he was the strategist. The poor old soldiers never got a look in!

Here is a summary of the four 2D-management competences and their impact on the 'assistants'.

COMPETENCE 1 • FORMULATING CLEAR TARGETS

Depending on his vision and strategy, the 2D-manager was capable of formulating clear targets for every one of his team members. He was not alone is this: the specialists in organisational development created the necessary systems for him. Perhaps the most well known of these mechanisms was the concept of the 'SMART objectives', which was so well received back in those 2D-days. In fact, SMART is still a favourite subject in the curriculum for new managers. Goals or assignments are SMART if they meet the following requirements:

- Specific: the assignment has to be well defined and clearly formulated.
- Measurable: the result can be measured and evaluated.
- Acceptable: the 2D-employees accept the goals and work towards them.
- Realisable: the assignment needs to be possible; it should neither be too hard or too easy.
- Time-bound: the assignment will be completed (someday).

Within this framework, the 2D-employees adapted to the 2D-manager. They were required to be obedient. The mutually-agreed upon goals gave direction to this obedience and deviation from the goals was only possible after discussion with the manager. The 'best' employees made sure that the annually agreed upon goals were reached.

It was in this way that situations were created where employees only needed half of their working hours to accomplish their set goals: for the rest of the time, they occupied themselves with trivia. They were experts in camouflaging their idleness but were shining examples of 'good' employees to the 2D-manager. They made sure that his spreadsheet of goals and objectives were achieved. This kind of employee behaviour was only possible because it was almost impossible for the 2D-manager to control all his team members. He was satisfied when he was able to complete his administration and tick off the goals in the spreadsheet during annual reporting meetings.

It goes without saying that clear arrangements need to be made about 'who does what' in a well-oiled 2D-organisation. Consequently, the formulation of crystal clear job descriptions was part of the capable 2D-manager's essential skill set. The job description contained a list of tasks which the candidate-employee could or had to do. Together with the organisational chart, these tasks were the reinforcing steel rods in the concrete of the organisation. The best systems also had a classification system which defined the size of the salary. This is how the salary spreadsheet was gradually set up.

Good job descriptions also made it possible to find new employees quickly. Over the years, the job description was used as a tool to develop the 2D-manager's job as well. All this was perfected by the 2D-HR department.

It was also drummed into the team members (or assistants) that they had to perform all aspects of a job, whether they liked it or not. The strict definition of functions in job descriptions often resulted in situations where members of 2D-teams did not support one another. Why should they? After all, it was not their job to take over a colleague's tasks (for instance, if he was sick). As a manager in a 2D-organisation, I saw how human resources were squandered by the combination of targets and jobs descriptions. A 2D-team member stubbornly kept to the limits of his task list and his job description. So much for flexibility!

The best 2D-managers didn't just occupy themselves with targets and job descriptions; they evolved into managers who guided their employees through their own personal development. They searched for and found the necessary education for their subordinates. In general, it was the annual performance monitoring meeting which gave guidance to this 'coaching' process. 2D-managers consulted with their employees and discussed deficiencies or weaknesses that they had observed. Agreements about training courses would follow. The result was discussed again the next year. Sometimes. More often than not, there was a catch: most courses were organised or attended because "it was obligatory". Most of the time there was no genuine, mutual commitment to learn between 2D-managers and their team members. Not surprisingly, the results of these courses left a lot to be desired.

There is something else here, too: the 2D-manager's attitude towards the transfer of information was regarded at the time as being 'praiseworthy'. After all, it was his mission to give his assistants *only* the information that was needed to complete the allocated tasks. In this way, the 2D-manager made sure that his employees were not inundated with information. He was the information filter – and why not? He was the expert, wasn't he? I can illustrate this with an anecdote.

During a seminar about organisational development, I once asked a group of 2D-managers why they didn't allow their employees to choose courses for themselves. Their answer was unanimous: it was too risky because there was a possibility that they would choose the wrong course... This kind of attitude leads to the wrong kind of results: one day an employee asked me: "Why do I need to take a course that I don't need and why don't I ever get to take a course that I *do* need?" It was a good question, to which I could only reply with a grimace.

COMPETENCE 4 • DELEGATING RESPONSIBILITIES

It is this final competence that truly marks someone out as a 2D-manager. How did he manage to keep his employees busy without constantly breathing down their necks? If he could achieve this, the self-managing team was almost within reach.

The technique referred to as 'situational leadership' is known by almost everyone nowadays. Just look on the Internet and you will find a deluge of information about it. The underlying idea behind this technique is that employees who can handle their tasks and execute them well do not need to be permanently supervised. You can just let them get on with their job.

If a 2D-employee reached this level, he was usually ready to be promoted to a position as a 2D-manager in the 2D-organisation. Loyalty, faultless execution and intellectual obedience were the criteria. It was from this group of employees that the next generation of 2D-managers was picked – the incubator for 2D-talent, the 2D-high potentials.

The manager who possessed these four competences was part of a select group of 2D-manager prodigies. After all, he had 'pulled it off' and got strong results with his team in the 2D-era. In fact, they were the ideal 2D-team.

It was clear to these managers that they needed to be more than just experts in their chosen field, if they wanted to lead a team. For this reason, they evolved into the so-called 'friendly' experts. Managing by fear or terror was not their style. They knew that this would only cause problems and put stress on the team. To distinguish this group of 2D-managers from the others, the concept of a 'people manager' was introduced. These people were 2D-managers who did not just belong to the elite in their field of expertise, but were also capable of motivating a team in such an elegant and humane manner that the team would execute their tasks with enthusiasm. Even today, these capabilities are highly valued by human resource managers when they are looking to recruit new managers. In short, the 2D-manager has to strike a balance between motivating his team to achieve operational success on the one hand, while continuing to excel as the 'best expert' in the team's field of expertise on the other hand.

THE 2D-MANAGER AS RED MONKEY BREEDER: FACT OR FICTION?

This harsh judgement which we have just passed on the 2D-manager does need some clarifying. There was once a time when the 2D-manager could even consider himself to be a Red Monkey Breeder.

Owing to his technical superiority, he was the driving force behind every innovation. He launched new ideas, releasing Red Monkeys in the work environment on a regular basis – and because of his authority, no one dared to shoot them.

He evaluated his team members' creative ideas on the basis of their feasibility and approved them or not. His position as chief expert was not contested, largely because he was able to predict with accuracy the impact of every new idea. However, the ideas which the 2D-manager was unable to understand clearly never stood a chance.

I remember this form of management from the time when I was still working as an engineer. My manager was the 'smartest' engineer and thus we respected him. He motivated us and if we had a technical problem, he would always help us to solve it. In his function he was an expert for 80% of the time and a manager for 20%. For him, this was 20% too much (he didn't like being a manager), but it was part of his job description – and so he did it. There was nothing wrong with his way of managing. It worked perfectly in the 2D-era.

Whether this still holds good in a 3D-organisation remains to be seen: so let us now look at the necessary competences of the 3D-manager.

The 3D-manager's competences

In figure 10, the required competences of the 3D-manager are set alongside to those of the 2D-manager. It gives us the following comparison:

- Formulating targets 'becomes developing' a vision or Visioning.
- Completing job descriptions becomes Casting (casting is a concept from the world of cinema and theatre, where the right actor is picked or 'cast' for the right part).

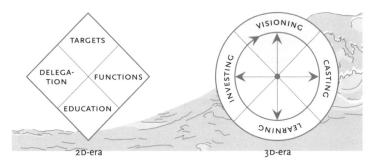

Figure 10 · *The new competences of the 3D-manager compared with the old competences of the 2D-manager*

- Organising training courses becomes 'launching lifelong learning' or Learning.
- Delegating responsibilities becomes making budgets and resources available, or Investing.

The 2D-manager's talents, which are primarily based on technical expertise, are unfit for this kind of stressful job. In the 2D-era, the 2D-manager was in control at any given moment. He stood on the bridge of his ship, knew all its secrets and could predict far in advance the course it had to take. But just like the captain of the *Titanic,* he did not see the treacherous icebergs which litter the globalised ocean of the rapidly evolving technical world. His biggest weakness is his status as an expert, a status which he has to maintain by improving his expertise every day. This is a time-consuming battle that the 2D-manager is bound to lose. The 2D-manager's desire to remain an expert and to control his team accordingly is a disaster in the 3D-era.

This is why the 3D-manager encourages his employees to be (or perhaps they already are) smarter than himself. They are the real experts now. The 3D-manager's job is 'simply' to guarantee that his team will execute a mission. In this respect, painting a team vision and strategy is his first and most important task. After all, in the 3D-era organisations need to innovate faster and faster. They can only succeed in doing this if every team member is closely involved in the innovation process. The guiding energy which motivates the team members has at its source a gripping vision and strategy – and this is the work of the 3D-manager. Defeatist 2D-managers will never believe in this. They think that such an approach leads directly to chaos. They find it unthinkable that employees have the freedom to come up with their own innovative ideas by themselves. The 3D-manager makes sure that this is precisely what happens. In fact, his entire management style is based on it. He knows that thanks to his competences of Visioning, Casting, Learning and Investing, a new balance will be created – a process we will now look at in more detail.

AGILITY AND THE ENGINE OF INNOVATION®

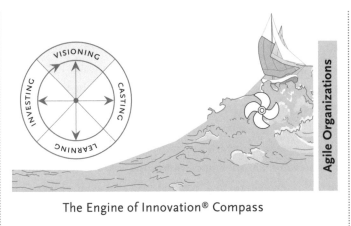

The Engine of Innovation® Compass

Figure 11 · *The Engine of Innovation® compass helps 3D-organisations to find the right direction*

The competences of 3D-management we call agility competences. 'Agility' literally means 'being nimble'. There seems to be a hint of magic about it, but in fact there is nothing magical about it at all: it's just a skill like any other – a flexibility of thinking and acting. 3D-organisations need nimble managers and employees, because they are very agile and can quickly react to any change. In the 3D-era, this manoeuvrability is absolutely essential to power the organisation's Engine of Innovation and to quickly adjust the course to the chosen direction. The circle that symbolizes the four agility competences is called the Engine of Innovation Compass.

AGILITY COMPETENCE 1 • DEVELOPING A VISION,
OR VISIONING

Predicting the future is difficult: continuously spotting new trends and predicting their impact on the team and the organisation is the manager's hardest task of all. In fact, it will become too much for many managers. The 3D-manager will realise this and will surround himself with employees with whom he can freely discuss these matters. The manager will be the indispensable link with top management. Together with his team members, he translates the organisation's vision into a vision for his team.

This team vision provides the mental force which combines and focuses each team member's individual input. The best description of this force might be a "passionate driving commitment". The vision is intuitive, because newly anticipated trends will require quick adjustments to both the vision and its resultant strategy. Employees are actively involved in formulating these adjustments.

This is why the 3D-manager surrounds himself with 3D-employees who, fired by their common passion for realising the vision, impose goals on themselves: not because they have to, but because they want to. They want to realise the vision with the same passion as their 3D-manager. The 3D-HR department will implement 3D-processes to help 3D-managers and 3D-top managers to develop different team visions within the organisation. A lively dialogue between employees, top managers and middle managers is created through these processes and the resultant dialogue ensures that the different teams *and* the organisation itself adapt constantly.

This creates a self-guided organisation with one single, overriding goal: realising the vision.

> *3D-organisations do not have one vision; they have a chaotic mixture of different team visions, which form a coherent whole when viewed from a distance.*

It must be understood that this vision is never fully realised, just like the fictitious point on the horizon is never actually reached. Time and again, the 3D-manager adds new elements to the vision. His team understands this subtle game: after all, it is co-responsible for the vision. The team members get their satisfaction from the results they achieve. Their passion remains and even increases, because they want to travel the full length of the path, with all its unexpected twists and turns.

3D-managers differ substantially from their 2D-colleagues, because they no longer think in terms of tasks. The problem with tasks in the 3D-era is that they very quickly become outdated. Consequently, the 3D-manager thinks instead in terms of an endless vision-energy source, which inspires his team to formulate their own mission. The 3D-manager who goes on vacation leaves behind him a team which can continue its work without interruption, thanks to the energy it derives from the collectively created vision. A 2D-manager who has been away for a while *knows* that his team will eventually come to a halt and that it will only finish the specific tasks which he set them before he left.

Contrary to what 2D-managers often think, the 3D-manager *does* act firmly. Employees who are not interested in the collective vision of the team are quickly given another place which *does* interest them – either inside or outside the organisation. The 3D-manager owes this to himself, to the team and to the employee.

AGILITY COMPETENCE 2 • CHOOSING THE RIGHT EMPLOYEES, OR CASTING

Developing an inspiring vision is just the first competence of the 3D-manager; picking the right cast is his second most important task. If his vision can be compared to a film script which he wants to act out , his second job as 'director' is to create the best possible team. He does not necessarily need all his team members/actors at the same time. Some actors only play a part at the beginning, in the middle or at the end of the movie; others get a starring role and remain on set for almost the entire film. This particular script has one major difficulty, however: it is still being written while the movie is being shot.

This is why the 3D-manager does not always work with the same actors. His team will probably have a permanent core, but just like in a TV soap there are plenty of guest actors. They are given a part which corresponds to the intended outcome of the vision. Casting has an important place in the mental model of the team and its work. A good 3D-manager must act as a talent scout. He looks for passionate employees who can contribute to the team's mission and vision. He expects his 3D-employees to truly *live* their part. He will coach them, if necessary, but if he feels that an employee does not have enough passion or talent, he will not hesitate to get rid of him.

> 3D-*managers are looking for the right talents and* 3D-*employees are looking for the right role.* 3D-*organisations make sure that they find each other.*

Bad casting is detrimental to all concerned; both for the 3D-employee and for the team's performance. 3D-employees understand this and realise that their rejection is not personal but is more a matter of the team's need for the right person, at the right time, in the right place. A 3D-employee is never a "bad worker". At most, he was poorly cast. The 3D-manager always needs to be able to enlist help from the organisation's 3D-HR department. Employees must be able to work for different managers within this kind of structure. Consequently, the evaluation and reward system has to be based on a flexible form of organisation. This could never work in an organisation of reinforced concrete: in other words, in a 2D-organisation.

Managers and employees in the 3D-organisation do not see talent development as a matter of attending so many 'successful' courses. Talent development is the result of the casting process. Employees are coached, as it were, towards the roles with which they can challenge their own talents. This heightens their learning motivation to master new business competences. The casting is not forced upon them. It is almost as if they ask for a specific role, so that they can expand their talents.

Nowadays, talent is more highly valued than a university degree. In the 3D-organisation, the manager no longer 'owns' the employees, as was often the case in the 2D-era. He uses their talents to clear the path towards the vision. Here, too, he acts firmly. Badly cast team members will be replaced as quickly as possible.

AGILITY COMPETENCE 3 • LIFELONG LEARNING OR LEARNING

The 3D-manager gives his employees enormous freedom to learn. Moreover, the employees can also decide how best to use this freedom. After all, what does the manager have to lose? Passionate employees who support a common vision are always inclined to use their talents to realise that vision. Consequently, the manager does not want to stand between them and the information they need.

Because the 3D-manager is aware that he is living in the 3D-era, knowledge and information are allowed to flow rapidly. He understands that society itself is constantly changing. This change is so rapid that his employees need to learn almost continuously, in order to keep doing their jobs well. The manager does not have to check up on them, because their motivation is inspired by the solid foundations of vision and casting.

The fear of abuse (and subsequent anarchy) which characterised the 2D-manager is unknown to the 3D-manager, provided he has developed his first two competences carefully and responsibly. If each member of his team is provided with challenging tasks which closely correspond to their own intrinsic talents, they will accept these tasks with passion. As a result, the tasks in question will automatically augment their talents still further. When this happens, an employee acquires new insights which help him reach his goals more quickly and more efficiently. Creative, challenging ideas are the almost inevitable result. Red Monkeys spontaneously come to life in people who are passionate about their role and have access to the right information. This is where the natural innovation process – the process which we have called the Red Monkey Innovation Process – actually begins. One idea sparks another...

The 3D-manager is in complete harmony with his team members, each of whom decides independently about the route of their learning journey. Meanwhile, he also encourages them to learn from one another and to challenge each the others with new insights. He talks continuously about the vision and constantly shows his employees that the vision and its related strategy are the team's driving forces. Thanks to these powerful motivating forces, everyone is able to develop his talent; not as a result of competing with one another, but as a result of learning together.

Learning in 3D-organisations does not happen because it is obligatory, but because it is allowed.

2D-managers believe that if new employees spend too much time on 'learning', they will no longer 'work' properly. Nothing could be further from the truth. Employees who are driven by a passion to realise a challenging vision consider learning to be a necessary condition to the more rapid achievement of that vision. They have a strong sense of responsibility and a strong desire to put into practice what they have learned.

By looking at a team's learning process, you can see whether the 3D-manager is the right man for the job. If he worries too much about what his employees will do with their freedom to learn, it is obvious that he has not sufficiently mastered his Visioning and Casting competences. Managers who do not allow their employees to buy books or do not give them access to the Internet clearly have a problem. The competent 3D-manager, who carries out his visioning and casting in the 3D-world, should not have any difficulties with this. He knows that he has created order in the chaotic process we call 'learning'.

Margaret J. Wheatley made a fascinating observation on this subject: "People are afraid and frustrated when they use the thinking pattern of problem-solving to find a way out of the chaos. But we do not allow this. We let them generate even more information. Eventually, they will let go and just at that moment, they present courageous solutions which take all relevant information into account."

Human resources departments must cut all ties with their traditional education processes if they want to adapt to the 3D-management style. For example, how does an annual training programme or a competence management system align with the 3D-manager's frame of reference? Or how can the HR-department calculate the return on investment, if 80% of all learning processes in the 3D-organisation are informal? Nowadays, the HR department does not even know when or how the employees are actually learning!

And what about collective agreements which state that a percentage of the salary budget must be earmarked for traditional courses? How should the department react if these agreements are counterproductive for both the organisation and its 3D-employees? In this context, it is worth noting that the unions should rethink their policies with regard to lifelong learning.

3D-managers, 3D-employees and 3D-HR departments all need to work together to create an informal, self-guiding learning environment. Thus learning becomes a natural process, integrated into the job, just like process innovation. It could be called 'Total Learning Management', analogous to 'Total Quality Management'.

AGILITY COMPETENCE 4 • MAKING BUDGETS KNOWN AND AVAILABLE OR INVESTING

This is the 3D-manager's ultimate test and also the biggest obstacle for many aspiring managers. What is the entire point of a 3D-organisation? In short, it is designed to give 3D-employees the opportunity to put into actual practice the things which they have learned. And if Learning drives creativity, Investing drives the spirit of entrepreneurship. This is the key factor which ensures innovation in the workplace.

3D-employees are responsible for the tools which they use to translate their ideas into practice. This can be compared to the athlete whom we mentioned earlier. In a 3D-environment, he acquires his own budget to buy his own equipment and to invest in his own infrastructure.

The 3D-manager should always be open and honest with his employees. This means that he must share information about the budgets available for change and innovation. A 3D-employee who is aware of the budgetary parameters feels more closely involved in the innovation process of which he is a part. He gears his proposals and ideas to reflect budgetary limitations. If he doesn't know the size of the budget, he may launch unrealistic proposals or keep good ideas to himself, simply because he does not know whether they are financially feasible. 'Insight' and 'involvement' are the investing 3D-manager's key words.

> *Investing is the process of giving tools and resources to employees, who can then decide for themselves what to do with them. It is the ultimate test for 3D-managers.*

This is a huge taboo for the 2D-manager. In a 2D-Organisation, he is the only person who knows the available budgets. At most, he will sometimes remark that there is "still some money left", preferably near the end of the financial year, and only then because all the money must be spent, otherwise he would 'lose' it. In contrast, the 3D-manager realises that 3D-employees who are aware of budget details might be more inclined to look even harder at the proposed changes, in the hope of realising them at a lower cost. In this scenario, the employee has evolved from a passive follower to a creative entrepreneur. From now on, innovation starts in the workplace!

As with the human resources department, the organisation's financial department will also need to ally itself with the 3D-manager. Which investment processes need to change, in order to help the

3D-managers to meet the challenge of constant innovation? Is it enough to have just one annual budget distribution? Can more flexible ways of redeploying resources be developed?

The 3D-manager has sustainable intelligence

During my career as training manager and Corporate Learning Officer, I often wondered what the profile of the new 3D-manager should be. I came up with the following definition: "3D-managers are talented in managing teams". But this leads to further ques-

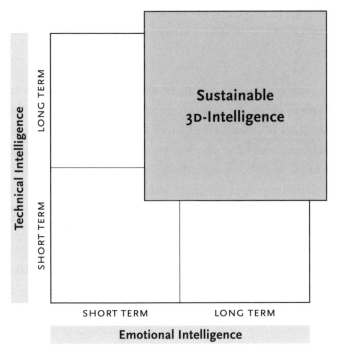

Figure 12 · *Sustainable intelligence results in sustainable 3D-organisations*

tions. What is management talent? How do you discover it? How do you give it opportunities? How do you use it?

This was clear in 2D-organisations: a talented manager was a technically superior expert who could realise 2D-goals with his team. But this kind of talent will not suffice in the 3D-era. A 3D-manager no longer has to be *the* technical expert. Besides, this is virtually impossible nowadays. Consequently, everyone in the team will need to be an expert to a certain extent in one or more specific subjects. The most important thing for the 3D-manager is his ability to use his agility competences (Visioning, Casting, Learning and Investing), in order to guide his team and make it work together towards the vision which he has proposed and the entire team has accepted.

These agility competences cannot always be taught: you are 'born with them'. They are an integral part of the 3D-manager's intelligence. This is an entirely different kind of intelligence than the intelligence which the 2D-manager used to support his 'empire'. The 3D-manager has to make decisions based on a long-term vision. Not everything can be predicted with spreadsheets and charts. He has to make correct decisions using his intuition and relatively little information. I call this 'creative entrepreneurship'.

Intuitive action – not being able to explain something but still being correct – is one of the most important characteristics of a 3D-management talent. 2D-managers dismiss intuitive long-term thinking as "dreaming". To them, continuous improvement is the best way to stay ahead of the game. As a result, they get bogged down in short-term thinking. I have illustrated this difference in figure 12.

The 3D-manager "sees" connections between activities and processes, using his sustainable intelligence. Moreover, he does this for both the short-term and the long-term, and in relation to both emotional and technical issues. Let's look at this more closely and compare the different management competences which we have already discussed.

VISIONING AND SUSTAINABLE INTELLIGENCE

The manager has the competence to distil a long-term vision for his team, based on the input of his team members and the organisation. This means he is capable of forming a mental image of the desired future, taking different trends and possible changes into account. This could be called his 'long-term intelligence'.

But that's not all. At the same time, he must also ignite the necessary passion in his workers, so that they can realise this future image together. This will not happen simply by giving them tasks; he must have an emotional long-term vision. Tasks do not have to be completed by a certain deadline because that is how the manager has planned it, but because the employee is driven enough to want to complete his tasks *himself*. That is how a modern 3D-manager must work.

CASTING, LEARNING AND INVESTING

Again, the 3D-manager should take into account a long-term vision and strategy, in order to achieve the right balance of Casting, Learning and Investing. His long-term vision should both be technical and emotional, and his strategy should be based strongly on the use of intuition.

He constantly casts people in new roles so they can – are obliged to – prove themselves over and over again. He challenges them to learn new competences spontaneously, hoping that they will use them in other fields of endeavour. And most dangerous of all: he will invest in his team without being sure whether his investment will yield profits. The combination of his technical and emotional intelligence leads to a newer, more powerful 'sustainable intelligence'. We have to regard managers in the 3D-era as talented professionals who in the first place can manage people. The complexity of modern management processes will force organisations to scout for people with actual 3D-management competences. It becomes a quest for management talent.

In the 2D-era this was not necessary. A manager was just a technical expert, with management tacked on as his second job. In the 3D-era he is now a management expert with some technical knowledge. We are seeing a complete re-evaluation of middle management.

Most 2D-managers will not succeed in transforming themselves into 3D-managers. This is probably the most painful conclusion for many companies, as they try to evolve from a 2D-organisation to a 3D-organisation. A 2D-organisational culture cannot be transformed into a 3D-organisational culture simply by making their 2D-managers do their jobs better. As a result, the 2D-manager will become an endangered species; the 3D-manager is a completely different being from a totally different part of the jungle!

3D-management is not the result of competence management and education; it is the result of scouting talent and giving opportunities for competence development.

Stop the anarchy!

Everything I have mentioned so far about the 3D-manager and the 3D-employee is like a red rag to a bull for the 2D-managers, because they do not understand the concept of sustainable intelligence. They will fight to the bitter end – which not only means their own end but also possibly their organisation's end. I have not named this section "Stop the anarchy!" for nothing. It is the most common cry of 2D-managers and 2D-HR departments, who are convinced that they have to stop the evolution towards a 3D-organisation. Some of the arguments they use include:

- "Employees cannot make their own decisions about what they need to learn, because this would lead to anarchy. They would only choose to learn the things that they like." During a lecture on empowerment, a senior manager (a CEO) dismissed the entire idea as completely unfeasible. He did not trust a single person from amongst his thirty employees when he was absent. To him, empowerment was an unrealistic utopia: something for 'softies' and totally impractical in a business environment.
- "Access to the Internet at work has to be strictly controlled. If this does not happen, employees will do nothing but surf the worldwide web. They will neglect their work and their performance will plunge." I once suggested to a company that they should get rid of the company library and let employees keep the books they ordered. To the 2D-manager of human resources, this was sheer blasphemy. "If we allowed that, employees would buy books for their spare time at home," he fumed. Near the end of the 1990s, I installed a video network in a company, with the help of the Director of Research & Development. Employees could watch

videotapes about technical matters but also about general topics. There was a big fear in the 2D-HR department that all employees would leave their work and only watch the tapes!

- "Following a classic training course is not a problem, is it? At least this gives some measure of control. If employees become members of a network or learn online, there is almost no control at all."

2D-managers and 2D-HR departments are always afraid of losing control. To them, this leads inevitably to a state of pure anarchy. If they don't keep a tight leash on their employees, some form of lawlessness and abuse is bound to break out – or so they reason. But is it really like that? Or do they simply lack insight into how to manage in a different way?

There was a time when we learned to fall, so that we could later be able to walk. 2D-managers have forgotten this.

2D-managers are confronted with a very difficult choice. Do they remain super athletes, like the Belgian cyclist Eddy Merckx, who always wanted to be the first and the best? Or are they prepared to take up the challenge of being a 3D-manager?

John Cleese put it perfectly in one of his management training videos. In one of the scenes, a manager asks whether he should encourage his employees to learn, because he is afraid that they will become so smart that they will eventually want to leave his team. Cleese answered: "What do you want? To be the manager of a bunch of incompetent employees or to be the manager of a bunch of very competent employees, one of whom will leave every now and then, because he wants a bigger challenge?" The expression on the manager's face was obvious: you could see him thinking "What about me? What happens to me if my employees become smarter than I am? How can I avoid anarchy if I am not the smartest and don't have everything under control? What role will I play in this new situation?" And tears welled up in the manager's eyes, because he knew that he did not want to – or perhaps never could be – a 3D-manager.

2D-managers resist the transition to the 3D-era. They use emotionally-loaded words like 'anarchy' and 'abuse' to support their doom-mongering. They have lost the stable balance that they were easily able to maintain in the 2D-organisation and from *that* point of view, they are completely right – but their point of view is totally outdated. 3D-managers know this and see things differently. They *do* see a balance in the new 3D-era, even if it is a chaotic balance. It is the balance of constant innovation.

Conclusion: the compass of the 3D-manager

3D-managers get things done 'easily'. Not once, but every time. Thanks to the development of his four 3D-agility competences, the 3D-manager achieves considerable results: the Red Monkey Innovation Processes is making progress.

These 3D-managers create the right mindset and conditions for the creators and the pioneers to start the almost endless breeding of Red Monkeys. Motivation, involvement and passion are the key elements in their strategy. As a result, the innovative learning organisation develops a natural innovation process.

Anarchy, abuse, chaos and all the other arguments which the 2D-manager uses to shield himself have no effect in the true 3D-organisation. Even the seeming randomness of creative and intuitive entrepreneurship is not really chaos, because it contains an implicit balance: a chaotic balance that is realised by a new management generation – the generation of 3D-managers. This balance is achieved by Visioning, Casting, Learning and Investing, the four key agility competences which fuse together into the Engine of Innovation Compass.

In 3D-organisations, innovation starts with all the employees of whatever level who have the talents and competences to truly innovate. At that moment, a continuous stream of challenging ideas starts to flow, a self-fuelling process of perpetual motion, as it were. One idea leads to another. This creates an apparently chaotic influx of Red Monkeys – but chaos is not always what it seems. The Red Monkeys are shared with all the interested pioneers in the organisation and are able to grow. This is called Total Innovation Management and it is the true meaning of 3D-balance. We will discuss this further in chapter 10.

10 Total Innovation Management: a new concept

Introduction

Innovation is a natural process. Darwin taught us that nature continuously reinvents itself. It does this at a snail's pace, practically invisible to the naked eye. Only if you look at the world and the changing appearance of our planet 'throughout the centuries', will you be able to see the changes. During this long history some species have disappeared, while others have adapted to new habitats. In some cases, completely new species have evolved, because the circumstances were just right for their arrival. At the same time, we now also know that nature does not 'innovate' when there is no reason to do so. This has been shown by the recent discovery of primordial fish at the bottom of the ocean which are no different

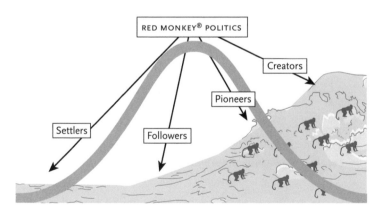

Figure 13 · *In nature a balance exists between creators and settlers*

from their prehistoric ancestors. Even nature has its settlers. This 'nature' metaphor might not be perfect, but it helps us to better understand 3D-innovation and the reasons why 2D-organisations have such difficulty to innovate.

If we look at the actors in the innovation proposition as portrayed in figure 13, we can see that the levels of creators, pioneers, followers and settlers are roughly the same as in 'nature'.

There is a natural distribution that calmly guides the innovation process. Because there is no real threat, this natural process does not provide a large number of creators; and the relatively few creators have nothing to fear from the similarly small group of settlers.

Innovation stagnation in the 2D-organisation

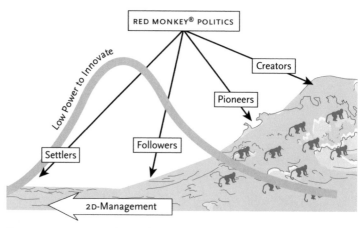

Figure 14 · *In 2D-organisations settlers are in power and creators are almost never seen*

During its development, an organisation *appears* to go through a 'natural' process but this is not the case. An organisational culture is not natural at all. People are 'gathered', in order to produce something. Depending on management style or management competences, different organisations will behave differently. An important consequence of the management style is the extent to which an organisation is capable of innovating and adapting to its environment.

Figure 14 illustrates how 2D-management in a 2D-organisation has mortgaged innovation. Top-down innovation processes – where innovation only starts at the 2D-management level – distorts the natural distribution of the company's population. In short, this means that the number of potential creators and pioneers is vastly decreased, when compared with the 'standard' natural distribution. Delays in the Red Monkey Innovation Process will inevitably result.

THE FIRE OF PASSION IS EXTINGUISHED

Organisations where 2D-management has destroyed the natural distribution of its employee population are tottering at the brink of disaster. At the time when their environment is moving rapidly toward the 3D-era, a lot of 'small' changes can push the organisation over the edge of the chasm that much faster.

Typical of this scenario are the small 2D-family businesses which were founded by Red Monkey Breeders. These breeders promote the growth of their company and keep the innovating role in their own 2D-management hands. But this cannot go on for ever. The fire to come up with new ideas again and again is slowly extinguished and the organisation's innovation power starts to fade away. This is understandable because no one is ready (or able) to 'fuel the fire' or come up with challenging new ideas. At this moment, it becomes painfully clear to these 2D-managers that they never thought enough about succession and continuation. No one in the organisation has the same passion or vision for the future that they once had. Unintentionally, the breeder has built an organisation of followers, his children included. When they take over the company, it often becomes clear that they do not have the necessary vision power. They remain in charge, uninspired, until the business declines and finally dies. The 3D-era can be very harsh.

In the 2D-era these organisations were able to survive because of their successful products and services; or because of supporting tax incentives; or because they profited from the patents which they had once created. 2D-management ensured that the majority of employees did not feel involved in the daily business and health of the organisation. They were treated like followers – This meant that at the time when the organisation most needed them – at the start of the 3D-era – they became settlers. In short, 2D-management will reap what it has sowed. In the 3D-era, their 'old-fashioned' management style means the demise of the organisation. They have somehow managed to eradicate any remaining innovation power.

Innovation in the 3D-organisation: helping nature a 'little'

A natural distribution of employee population will not help a 3D-organisation either. Or to be more precise: a 3D-organisation does *not* look for natural distribution. On the contrary, it needs an accelerated Red Monkey Innovation Process, as shown in figure 15.

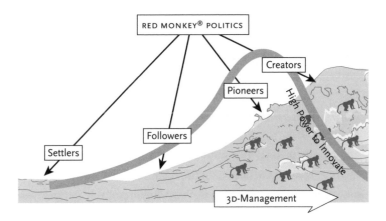

Figure 15 · *In 3D-organisations creators and pioneers realise a high power to innovate*

In other words, managers and top managers need to do everything in their power to turn the tide in the 3D-era. Organisations will only survive if they are able to drastically increase the number of Red Monkeys they produce. And this is only possible in a 3D-organisation with a 3D-management: these organisations make the Red Monkey Innovation Process work flat-out.

Employees need to be intimately involved in this process. They do not have to undergo it: they have to be an essential part of it. The rising influx of more and more Red Monkeys at the edge of the jungle and the introduction of Red Monkey Innovation Management makes surviving in the 3D-era much easier for the 3D-organisation. They become passionate about creative entrepreneurship again. The will and the urge to constantly innovate grow every day, sweeping along more and more employees. The number of creators increases and you will now find them at all levels in your organisation. Employees will make decisions about their own learning journeys and will always keep the goal and the vision of their team (and the organisation) in mind. The efforts that an organisation needs to make in order to establish this kind of perpetual creative growth we call Total Innovation Management.

Total Innovation Management

What exactly is Total Innovation Management? It is very simple. Everyone, from top to bottom of the organisation, is involved in the innovation process. Everyone plays an important role in empowering the Red Monkey Innovation Process. This did not happen in 2D-organisations in the 2D-era, nor was it possible: innovation was the exclusive preserve of management and its staff services. They were the only persons who had the information that was necessary to conceive innovative ideas. The 2D-manager served up innovation to his employees on a plate. All they had to do was swallow.

However, in the 3D-era the stream of information has become such a fierce, swirling river and the demand for innovative ideas is so urgent that 2D-management can no longer keep up with the pace. 2D-managers who want to keep everything under control are doomed to drown. The information stream – which should normally flow from the manager to his employees – shrinks to a tiny brook or dries up all together. The employees are confused, uninformed and 'settle'. The organisation slowly bleeds to death...

How can the 2D-organisation prevent this? It can only be done by encouraging employees to launch innovative ideas themselves. To do this however, the organisation must also give its employees the freedom to choose the information which is relevant to their current job and for the development of the new ideas.

If they do this, the information within the organisation no longer just flows from top to bottom , but pours through all possible channels and branches out in all directions. The organisation will consequently be 'forced' to transform into a 3D-organisation with 3D-managers – and these managers will need all their agility competences to supervise and steer everything along the right path: the path of the company vision.

The positive result is that the amount of challenging new ideas – Red Monkeys – will drastically increase. The organisation finally awakens from its COMA. Oxygen flows to its brain. The Red Monkey Innovation Process starts up again and the number of creators, pioneers and followers soars. A process of Total Innovation Management – which involves everyone – begins. Every employee is challenged to innovate at the workplace. Every employee can practice creative entrepreneurship and become a Red Monkey Breeder himself. Indeed, he is expected to become one!

Cultural change is not meant to transform all settlers and all followers into creators and pioneers; it is meant to tip the scales in favour of creators and pioneers.

Conclusion: long live the Red Monkey® Breeders!

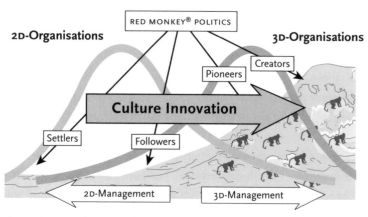

Figure 16 · *During the process of 3D culture innovation the balance shifts in favour of creators and pioneers. The Red Monkey® Innovation Process is started.*

2D-organisations survived in the 2D-era because their success was never contested. Even with a structural imbalance between creators and settlers (in favour of the settlers), resulting in the almost complete disappearance of the organisation's innovation power. There is only one possible way for these organisations to recover and once again become innovative in a sustainable manner: they have to kick-start the Red Monkey Innovation Process. This process ensures that the organisation's 'lost' or paralysed groups will reappear: creators or Red Monkey Breeders, with challenging new ideas; pioneers, who fine tune these ideas until they can be used; and followers, who understand the usefulness of the new ideas and want to use them.

The numbers of these groups must be increased drastically. In the 3D-era, not even a natural balance – with a limited number of creators and settlers facing a larger group of pioneers and a still larger group of followers – will suffice. The scales need to be tipped in favour of the creators and the pioneers.

The task of 3D-management is to ensure that the process of Total Innovation Management is properly implemented. To be able to achieve this, the organisation's management needs to work with conviction and perseverance in the direction of profound cultural change.

PART IV

....

CULTURE INNOVATION
AS A CONDITION FOR BUSINESS INNOVATION

11 Culture innovation

Introduction

Companies are so busy trying to set and achieve short-term business results that they have forgotten to think about the possible impact of a 3D-environment on their organisational culture. This is why most 2D-organisations have wandered into the 3D-era without any preparation and are now having to brave the turbulent waves of innovation in their unprepared barge. As the short-term challenges grow and intensify, so do the chances of survival diminish.

This is an important warning for 2D-organisations which are still successful today. They might not see the necessity of a quick turn-around to a 3D-organisational culture, even though they one day risk finding their 2D-ship in a violent 3D-storm. When this happens, it will be too late to bring about the life-saving culture change.

If a barge has to compete with a sailing boat equipped with a powerful engine on a quickly changing ocean, the barge will lose – and sink!

This chapter – in fact, this entire book – is a plea for 3D-culture innovation, for a transformation of the 2D-organisation into a 3D-organisation through a process of creative entrepreneurship. But what impact does culture innovation have on business innovation? We can illustrate this impact as a permanent circular motion: the 'Circle of Innovation'.

The Circle of Innovation

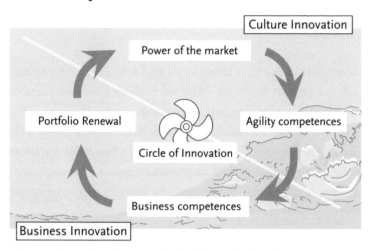

Figure 17 · *Innovation in the 3D-organisation is the result of a continuous process; the circle of innovation*

The circle of innovation is a process in which business and culture innovation are key elements. It is a circular motion, but with four distinct elements: (1) power of the market; (2) agility competences; (3) business competences; (4) portfolio renewal.

Figure 17 summarises this circular motion. If you can manage to set up this process and can ensure it continues to revolve, then business innovation should happen 'by itself', of its own volition.

Why? Because it has become a part of the organisation's genetic make-up.

GOAL: FAST BUSINESS INNOVATION

Fast business innovation allows an organisation to survive in a market that is changing very quickly. The speed of this business innovation is visible in the variety of the organisation's business portfolio.

PORTFOLIOS IN MOTION

When an organisation is active in highly competitive and innovative markets, the content of the organisation's catalogue of products and services – its portfolio – is an indicator of how fast it is evolving and following new trends.

For an outsider, the evolution of the portfolio is an indicator of the organisation's power to innovate. It shows the difference in turnover between products and services older than five years and more recent products and services. At least, that's how it used to be. In the 3D-era a renewal cycle of five years is much too slow; a period of two years or less will become the new standard. Older products in the portfolio go through a process of quick and continuous improvement, so that they can keep up for a while. But the demand for new products and services increases exponentially. Only creative entrepreneurship and innovation in the organisation's business processes can meet this demand.

Regularly updating the business portfolio is only possible if new business competences are routinely being developed. In this respect, the renewal of business competences can be viewed in the same light as the renewal of products and services: which business competences has the employee been using for more than five years and which have only recently been developed?. The faster the business competence portfolio renews itself, the more innovative the organisation will be.

The rate of renewal of the business competence portfolio is an indicator of an organisation's innovation power.

The following examples illustrate the meaning of business competences and their possible results:

- Engineers who have to master and use new technologies in order to regularly improve and innovate – technologies have to be sustainable and in balance with the world.
- Retirement homes which need employees who have mastered new techniques and processes to deal with an increasingly ageing population *and* to treat the 'customers' in a friendly manner. They need to master techniques which guarantee the same or an even better service.
- Employees who maintain good contacts with customers. They have 'off-the-record' conversations to develop new ideas. They no longer think of the customer with existing products and services in mind, but are constantly searching for new customer needs. These employees no longer maintain contacts based on demands but on conversations.
- Specialists who are faced with a technological revolution that never ceases. They will have to make non-stop efforts to keep up.
- Salesmen who regularly need to adapt their sales techniques to the changes taking place in the market.

- Bank clerks who are confronted by young people who are very familiar with online banking and online shopping.
- Journalists who need the latest communication techniques to keep in touch with breaking news stories.
- Teachers and lecturers who want to understand the world of their students and who need to develop new competences to create real, challenging learning environments.
- Unions who need to adapt to 3D-organisations. Their role in the 3D-era will also change constantly. Perhaps we need a 3D-union?
- Public servants who need insight into the world's complexity: otherwise they might implement outdated and inappropriate policies.

HUMAN CAPITAL IN A 3D-ENVIRONMENT

A company's employees are called its human capital. Today, the value of human capital is largely calculated by diplomas and other formal qualifications. In most cases, these also dictate the level of salary. In the future, such qualifications will contribute less to human capital appraisal. Instead, an employee's experience and agility competences will have more weight. The more his agility competences are developed, the faster he can develop the right business competences. It does not really matter anymore whether he has the right 'basic' diploma or not. The speed at which he can renew his business competence portfolio makes him a required talent – and a talent worth paying well.

To take part in the 3D-market game, organisations need to speed up the renewal time of their portfolio. They will only succeed in this task if they keep renewing their business competences – and this, in turn, can only succeed if they possess managers with the right agility competences.

Developing these vital agility competences is a far-reaching process, so that it cannot be achieved by simply trying to 'improve' 2D-organisations. 2D-culture improvement is no longer an option. What we need is the courage and the insight to transform the old 2D-organisational culture into a 3D-organisational culture. We need creative entrepreneurship in the field of culture development – before it is too late.

Culture innovation is creative entrepreneurship in culture development.

Consequently, culture innovation means the organic and accelerated break-up of 2D-management and 2D-HR processes, to be replaced by creative entrepreneurship in the field of culture development. The organisation will only able to develop its business competences at high speed and in a focused manner by cultivating the four agility competences: Visioning, Casting, Learning and Investing.

VISIONING

The development of a captivating and challenging vision serves to engage employees emotionally in the creation of a strategy to realise this vision. This gives direction to the business competences which need to be developed.

CASTING

Employees are cast in roles which – as far as possible – reflect their specific talents. This gives a huge boost to the employees' motivation, encouraging them to learn the necessary new business competences.

LEARNING

In the new environment, employees are challenged to learn 'how to learn'. They very consciously develop new learning competences, in order to quench (in a specific manner) their thirst for knowledge at the information tidal wave. This need for information puts them on the road to creativity: the road to new and challenging ideas. The subsequent development of new business competences is then inevitable.

INVESTING

Employees are encouraged to use their new knowledge and skills to take the initiative. Eventually, this will change their behaviour. They will no longer be passive followers, but will become active, creative entrepreneurs. This is true innovation in the workplace: Total Innovation Management.

The development of new business competences will result in real innovation. It is a process which continuously changes the contents of the organisation's portfolio in a very specific way.

THE DOUBLE DRAMA OF BUSINESS INNOVATION AND CULTURE INNOVATION

Business improvement and business innovation are two very different things. Business improvement is realised by continuously improving and developing the business competences or the technical competences of the organisation. Business innovation, however, is the result of dramatic interventions in the renewal of business competences. New business competences or technical competences are developed for this specific goal.

In the 3D-era, this renewal of business competences never stops; on the contrary, it accelerates. The organisation has to enter into a process of continuous business innovation by means of an unending renewal of business competences.

In the 3D-era, the 2D-manager can no longer keep up with the renewal of technical developments. He loses his authority as his team's 'main technical expert'. This is the first unpleasant fact he has to cope with. But there is more bad news: in the past the 2D-manager could always fall back on his 'second job' – that of a manager (as opposed to an expert). In fact, he became a manager *because* he was the technical expert.

In the 3D-era, this is no longer possible. Why not? Because the manager is no longer the expert. In this new era, he 'only' has to be a 3D-manager – and this role involves an entirely different set of responsibilities. Now he has to concentrate on the continuous development of the right business competences in his team. He does this by developing his own 3D-agility competences. If he fails to do this, the organisation will lose its fight against the competition, because its business portfolio is not renewed quickly enough, owing to the lack of the right business competences.

This leads to a second drama for the 2D-manager: the 3D-agility competences are so different from the competences needed for his old second-job-as-manager that he – and probably the majority of his colleagues – will not want to or will not be able to make the transition to 3D-management. This is particularly sad, because it is not really the 2D-manager's fault; it is the result of a normal evolutionary process in the 3D-environment.

All this is bad news for the many 2D-managers who might not be able or willing to give up their job, but who will lose their status as a manager. They will be replaced by new, vital wave of 3D-managers: a painful but necessary transition. If the organisation refuses to change the old 2D-guard, it only hurts itself and puts in jeopardy the transformation into a dynamic and battle-ready 3D-organisation.

A double dose of Red Monkey® Innovation Management

Organisations that really want to evolve into innovative and learning organisations are facing the enormous challenge of implementing a radical culture innovation process. It is the only option to survive in the long term. In the short-term they can survive by performing their core activities better than in the past. But there will come a day – and for many companies that day is creeping closer and closer, or may even have arrived – when a politics of improvement will no longer suffice. They will be forced to push through a serious business innovation programme but they will have to completely disrupt the organisational culture to do it.

Joel Baker, who we quoted in chapter 4, summarized this dilemma at one of his lectures: "'No one will thank you for taking care of the present if you have neglected the future."

Every organisation has its own creators, pioneers, followers and settlers. In the 2D-organisation the balance is weighted in favour of the settlers. To start accelerated Red Monkey Innovation Management for your business activities, you must also simultaneously start a programme of Red Monkey Innovation Management for your organisational development. Only then can a true 3D-organisation be created. And just like the business innovation process, so there will be creators, pioneers, followers and settlers, with all their usual conflicts. You will also be confronted with an organisational renewal war between Red Monkey Breeders and Red Monkey Hunters – and this battle will be vicious and bloody.

HIGH-RISK JOB IN CULTURE INNOVATION

The role of a Red Monkey Breeder is always a dangerous one, especially in organisations which still need to move away from their 2D-organisational culture. The chances of being injured or even killed by Red Monkey Hunters are very real.

However, there is a difference between Red Monkey Hunters in business innovation and in culture innovation. In business innovation, the game is rough but it is 'less personal' and 'less deadly'. In culture innovation, the struggle is bloody, because it is concerned with creative entrepreneurship in the structure and operation of the organisation. Those who dare to take on this job will soon be confronted with the sensibilities of the 2D-manager's 'status' or even with the wrath of the unions.

That is why I plead for the creation of a protected status for those who are responsible for the transition from 2D to 3D-organisations. It is the senior management's job to provide this protection. If this does not happen, Red Monkey Breeders will fall one by one.

It is worth remembering what Mark Twain once said: "At the beginning of change, the patriot is a scarce man: brave, hated and scorned. When his cause succeeds, the timid will join him – for then it costs nothing to be a patriot."

But whichever way you look at it, it is inevitable that the real transformation from a 2D-organisation into a 3D-organisation will be very stressful, involving as it does both Red Monkey Business Innovation Management and Red Monkey Culture Innovation Management.

Conclusion: first the ship, then the turbulent sea

An organisation in transition between the 2D-era and the 3D-era will meet two different kinds of Red Monkeys: those who will make the organisational culture tremble on its foundations and those who will disrupt the business portfolio.

Top managers need to understand that a permanent increase in the number of Red Monkeys – the only hope for meaningful business renewal – can only be achieved by efficient and effective Red Monkey Innovation Management for culture innovation.

The innovation circle connects all the different elements with impact on the power of an organisation to innovate. The power of the market will force the organisation to develop agility competences. These competences naturally accelerate the development of new and better business competences. At that moment, the creative entrepreneurship process also starts and the portfolio will quickly change to reflect the direction of the new organisational vision. The barge has been transformed into a ship that is now ready to face the stormy waters of the 3D-era.

Final conclusion · Red Monkey® Lovers

A new consensus...

Culture innovation is not always spontaneous. It is the result of a power struggle between the defenders of the 2D-era and the warriors of the 3D-era. But you cannot afford to wait until that battle is over or (even worse) simply "let things take care of themselves". You need to strive for a consensus about the necessity for real innovation.

I have been active in organisational development since 1988. In all those years, I have attended hundreds of lectures, conferences and discussions, listening to famous gurus as they argue how we must evolve from the 2D-era to the 3D-era. Yet most organisations are still stuck in the old days, while we are moving rapidly toward a new epoch.

An example of how old thinking and new problems confront each other can be seen in the way we treat global warming. We were warned of the horrendous consequences of this problem as early as the 1980s. Yet only now, when the dramatic effects are visible and provable, are governments and the business world finally prepared to do something about it. Unfortunately, they use measures which are largely rooted in 2D-models: with norms, goals and spreadsheets... There is not a single word about Visioning, Casting, Learning and Investing. Once again, it is a question of old wine in new bottles. The effects are probably not yet dramatic enough to initiate a truly radical culture change.

A couple of years ago, I gave a lecture about the necessity of changes in organisational cultures. After a passionate plea for the transition from the old management style to the new management style, I had lunch with some managers from a high-tech company. One of them asked me what I meant by Visioning, Casting, Learning and Investing. He did not understand it at all. Or rather, he thought that I was not telling him anything new, because he was already using these methods. I was surprised and asked him to clarify. He said, "I have a vision and I tell my employees what they have to do. There are clear job descriptions which are used for Casting. Everyone can follow training courses. We actually have a very broad educational programme. I think that covers Learning sufficiently. Finally, I give my employees responsibilities. I invest in them. So what is the problem?" The other people at the table nodded in agreement. At that moment, I realised how difficult it would be to convince successful 2D-organisations to ever change. I felt powerless and decided that a razor-sharp provocation was the only way to show this manager the error of his ways. After some hesitation, I asked him who was the 'smartest expert' in his team. His team consisted of about thirty highly skilled employees, but he did not need to think long before he answered: "I am". I immediately replied, "And that's exactly the problem." There followed an eerie silence. You can imagine how I felt: I stood alone facing a tight, united block of settlers. At that moment, I felt the real power of 2D-management.

But other people who were present reacted more positively. However, they too often felt powerless in the face of 2D-management strength, such as I had just experienced. After that lunchtime talk,

I decided that I had to provoke people more during my future seminars. Ever since that day, I no longer simply explain my theory, but also talk more about the impact which this theory can have on the daily practice of their organisations and on their own professional life. I tell the same story every time but frequently note large differences in the evaluations after the seminars. Sometimes the majority are willing to question their 2D-organisations, which usually leads to a series of constructive conversations about possible actions to build a 3D-organisation. But sometimes the majority are convinced that they are already working in a 2D-organisation. In these cases, conversations generally revolve around the fact that it is a 'bad' idea to give employees the freedom to choose their learning courses. In these situations it is clear that a constructive dialogue is virtually impossible.

The French writer Proust summarised this in one sentence: "The real voyage of discovery consists not in seeking new landscapes but in having new eyes."

... or a new conflict?

In this book you have been introduced to the concept of 'sustainable intelligence'. Sustainable intelligence in organisational development is the ability to see order in chaotic systems and to predict the long term consequences of these systems. Most people in management (at whatever level) do not have this talent. Yet this talent is essential for understanding the complexity of 3D-organisations and for promoting belief in your actions. The damaging division between believers and non-believers can only be resolved through a captivating vision and a clear strategy for culture innovation.

Striving for consensus is not enough. Innovation is never the result of consensus, but the outcome of a battle between Red Monkey Breeders and Red Monkey Hunters. Innovation is a conflict model. Culture innovation starts with a senior management which understands, believes and wants to shatter the status quo. It is willing to take risks and leads by example. Real innovation in organisational culture occurs when top management creates space for creative entrepreneurship. This serves to guarantee the security of those employees and managers who want to prove the validity and worth of the new vision.

The only necessary consensus is a consensus about the fact that conflicts are not just allowed, but are obligatory!

An organisation never evolves from a 2D-organisational culture to a 3D-organisational culture on the basis of consensus or 'democratic agreement'. Top management must be clear on this point but nonetheless needs to strive for a form of consensus in order to prevent conflicts from escalating out of control. Red Monkey Hunters need to understand that an organisation will not survive without innovation. Red Monkey Breeders need to accept that not everyone is ready to follow them blindly from the very first day. But this is the only consensus which is required. If there is agreement on these points, the double Red Monkey Innovation Process might just succeed. The human resources department has an important role to play. The old 2D-HR department was nothing more than a maintenance service for staff. The 3D-version is a service centre with a different strategic policy. Its role is so important that the human resources director needs to be part of the 3D-top management team, as a key strategic partner for the intended business innovation programme. The

3D-HR department's vision and strategy nourish the 3D-HR process-es and develop the competences which need to be achieved. This ensures proper insight into both the culture innovation process and the 2D-HR processes which need to disappear. The HR strategy is a plan to achieve organic evolution from a 2D-organisational culture to a 3D-organisational culture. It is a challenging plan, full of Red Monkeys – and it must succeed, if the organisation is to survive.

Challenging Red Monkeys

To conclude this book and to help you with your transition to a 3D-organisational culture, I will offer some illustrations of possible Red Monkeys in the field of culture innovation. They are challeng-ing, confrontational ideas, which might divide your organisation into Red Monkey Breeders and Red Monkey Hunters. Envisioning the possible implications of Red Monkeys on your organisational culture is a good exercise to try and understand the full complexity of the 3D-concept. Perhaps it is your first step in committing your-self to true 3D-management.

- Red Monkey: all degrees and other qualifications of employees and managers are deleted from the 3D-human resources data-base after five years.
- Red Monkey: the system of hierarchical and technical ladders is systematically removed.
- Red Monkey: 3D-employees have 'free time' to make themselves available for other projects in the organisation.
- Red Monkey: every 3D-manager must make the team vision available on the intranet for everyone in the organisation to read; anyone may react.

- Red Monkey: every 3D-employee gets a learning budget which he can spend in whatever way he wants.
- Red Monkey: no 3D-manager can continue to the end of his career as a 'manager'.
- Red Monkey: competence management systems do not matter in the 3D-organisation.
- Red Monkey: every 3D-employee maintains his own CV; this is available to everyone in the organisation.
- Red Monkey: all 3D-managers teach and coach a specific 3D-management competence.
- Red Monkey: every 3D-employee may attend a working meeting of another department.
- Red Monkey: employees who want to become a 3D-manager must first do this in a team where they have no technical knowledge about the team's tasks.
- Red Monkey: the learning history of 3D-managers and 3D-employees can be found on the intranet.
- Red Monkey: the learning strategy in a 3D-organisation should consist of employees and managers spending half their learning time 'learning from others' and the other half contributing to the learning process of others.
- Red Monkey: every employee has the opportunity to go to the edge of the jungle for themselves and...

Fill in your own new ideas. And if you think they are challenging enough, send them to me... or perhaps we might bump into each other on *www.redmonkey.be*. I would love to talk to you. Who knows, we might even do some Red Monkey business.

Thank you very much for reading this book and good luck with your life in the 3D-era...

MY ORGANISATION IS A JUNGLE